MALINOWSKI
COLLECTED WORKS

MALINOWSKI: COLLECTED WORKS

MALINOWSKI COLLECTED WORKS

VOLUME III

CRIME AND CUSTOM IN SAVAGE SOCIETY

Bronislaw Malinowski

London and New York

First published 1926 by Routledge

Reprinted 2002 by Routledge
2 Park Square, Milton Park, Abingdon, Oxon OX14 4RN

Simultaneously published in the USA and Canada
by Routledge
270 Madison Avenue, New York, NY 10016

Routledge is an imprint of the Taylor & Francis Group

Transferred to Digital Printing 2009

Typeset in Times New Roman by
Keystroke, Jacaranda Lodge, Wolverhampton

British Library Cataloguing in Publication Data
A catalogue record for this book is available from the British Library

Library of Congress Cataloging in Publication Data
A catalog record for this book has been requested

ISBN 0–415–21671–0 (set)
ISBN10: 0–415–26245–3 (hbk)
ISBN10: 0–415–48836–2 (pbk)

ISBN13: 978–0–415–26245–3 (hbk)
ISBN13: 978–0–415–48836–5 (pbk)

Publisher's Note
The publisher has gone to great lengths to ensure the quality of this
reprint but points out that some imperfections in the original book
may be apparent.

Fishing Canoes on the Lagoon.
(*See* page 18)

PLATE I.

Crime and Custom in Savage Society

By
BRONISLAW MALINOWSKI, D.Sc.
Author of *Argonauts of the Western Pacific*

LONDON
KEGAN PAUL, TRENCH, TRUBNER & CO. LTD.
BROADWAY HOUSE: 68–74 CARTER LANE, E.C.
1940

To

SIR RICHARD GREGORY, D.Sc.

Editor of *Nature*

CONTENTS

PART II

PRIMITIVE CRIME AND ITS PUNISHMENT

LIST OF ILLUSTRATIONS

PREFACE

THE modern anthropological explorer, who goes into the field fully trained in theory, charged with problems, interests, and maybe preconceptions, is neither able nor well-advised to keep his observations within the limits of concrete facts and detailed data. He is bound to receive illumination on matters of principle, to solve some of his fundamental difficulties, to settle many moot points as regards general perspective. He is bound, for example, to arrive at some conclusions as to whether the primitive mind differs from our own or is essentially similar ; whether the savage lives constantly in a world of supernatural powers and perils, or on the contrary, has his lucid intervals as often as any one of us ; whether clan-solidarity is such an overwhelming and universal force, or whether the heathen can be as self-seeking and self-interested as any Christian.

In the writing up of his results the modern anthropologist is naturally tempted to add his wider, somewhat diffused and intangible experiences to his

descriptions of definite fact ; to present the details
of custom, belief, and organization against the background of a general theory of primitive culture. This
little book is the outcome of a field worker's yielding
to such temptation. In extenuation of this lapse—
if lapse it be—I should like to urge the great need
for more theory in anthropological jurisprudence,
especially theory born from actual contact with
savages. I should also point out that in this work
reflections and generalizations stand out clearly from
the descriptive paragraphs. Last, not least, I should
like to claim that my theory is not made of conjecture
or hypothetical reconstruction but is simply an
attempt at formulating the problem, at introducing
precise concepts and clear definitions into the
subject.

The circumstances under which this thesis came into
being have also contributed towards its present form.
The material was first prepared and the conclusions
framed in response to an invitation from the Royal
Institution of Great Britain, before which a paper
was read (on the " Forces of Law and Order in
a Primitive Community ") on Friday evening,
13th February, 1925. As often happens, I found
myself with more material on my hands and many
more conclusions framed than could be included in
an hour's address. Some of these I have had the
privilege of publishing in *Nature* (see Supplement,

6th February, 1926, and article, 15th August, 1925). The full version is contained in this little book.

I wish to express my thanks to the Council of the Royal Institution for the kind loan of blocks and the permission to reproduce them. To Sir Richard Gregory, the Editor of *Nature*, I am indebted for allowing me to reprint the articles mentioned. I owe him much, moreover, for the help and encouragement I received from him in my earlier work.

In the preparation of this volume I received competent assistance from Mr. Raymond Firth, who is carrying on research work at the London School of Economics in the Department of Ethnology. I was able to secure his help through a grant from the Laura Spelman Rockefeller Memorial. The Board of this institution has of late devoted some special attention to the furtherance of anthropology, as a part of its interest in the development of the social sciences. The study of the rapidly vanishing savage races is one of those duties of civilization—now actively engaged in the destruction of primitive life—which so far has been lamentably neglected. The task is not only of high scientific and cultural importance, but also not devoid of considerable practical value, in that it can help the white man to govern, exploit, and "improve" the native with less pernicious results to the latter.

The Laura Spelman Rockefeller Memorial, through its enlightened interest in anthropology as a branch of the social studies, will earn a deep gratitude from present and future humanists in erecting a lasting monument to the noble woman in whose memory it has been founded.

B. M.

NEW YORK CITY.
March, 1926.

INTRODUCTION

ANTHROPOLOGY is still to most laymen and to many specialists mainly an object of antiquarian interest. Savagery is still synonymous with absurd, cruel, and eccentric customs, with quaint superstitions and revolting practices. Sexual licence, infanticide, head-hunting, couvade, cannibalism and what not, have made anthropology attractive reading to many, a subject of curiosity rather than of serious scholarship to others. There are, however, certain aspects of anthropology which are of a genuine scientific character, in that they do not lead us beyond empirical fact into realms of uncontrollable conjecture, in that they widen our knowledge of human nature, and are capable of a direct practical application. I mean such a subject, for example, as primitive economics, important for our knowledge of man's economic disposition and of value to those who wish to develop the resources of tropical countries, employ indigenous labour and trade with the natives. Or again, a subject such as the comparative study of the mental processes of savages, a line of research which has already proved fertile to psychology and might be made useful to those engaged in educating or morally improving the native. Last, but not least, there is the subject of primitive law, the study of the various forces which make for order, uniformity and cohesion in a savage tribe. The knowledge of these forces should have formed the foundation of anthropological theories of primitive organization and should have yielded the guiding principles of Colonial legislation and administration. A fuller knowledge of the so-called savages has revealed " Ye beastly devices of Ye heathen " as the product of firm law and of strict tradition, due to biological, mental and social needs of human nature, rather than as the outcome of unbridled passion and unfettered excess. Law and order pervade the tribal usages of primitive races, they govern all the humdrum course of daily existence, as well as the leading acts of public life, whether these be quaint and sensational or important and venerable. Yet of all branches of anthropology, primitive jurisprudence has received in recent times the scantiest and the least satisfactory treatment.

Anthropology has not always been so indifferent about savage justice and the methods of its administration as it is at present. About half a century ago there was a positive epidemic of research into primitive law, especially on the Continent, more particularly in Germany. It is enough to mention the names of Bachofen, Post, Bernhöft, Kohler and the other writers grouped round the *Zeitschrift für vergleichende*

Rechtswissenschaft to remind the sociologist of the scope, volume and quality of the work done by them. This work, however, was heavily handicapped. The writers had to rely upon the data of the early amateur ethnographers—modern field-work of the trained specialist, done with method, purpose and knowledge of the problems, was at that time not yet in existence. In an abstract and complex subject such as primitive law, amateur observations are on the whole useless.

The early German students of savage law again were all and one committed to the hypothesis of ' primitive promiscuity ' and ' group-marriage ', just as their British contemporary, Sir Henry Maine, was handicapped by his too narrow adhesion to the patriarchal scheme. Most of these continental efforts in anthropological jurisprudence were directed to—in fact, wasted upon—the task of proving that Morgan's theories were correct. The myth of ' group-marriage ' was casting its shadow on all their arguments and descriptions and it infected their juridical constructions with the kindred concepts of ' group-responsibility ', ' group-justice ', ' group-property ', and ' communism ', in short, with the dogma of the absence of individual rights and liabilities among savages.

Underlying all these ideas was the assumption that in primitive societies the individual is completely dominated by the group—the horde, the clan or the tribe—that he obeys the commands of his community, its traditions, its public opinion, its decrees, with a slavish, fascinated, passive obedience. This assumption, which gives the leading tone to certain modern discussions upon the mentality and sociality of savages, still survives in the French school of Durkheim, in most American and German works and in some English writings.

Thus handicapped by insufficient material and baseless assumptions, the early school of anthropological jurisprudence was driven into an impasse of artificial and sterile constructions. In consequence it proved incapable of real vitality, and the whole interest in the subject heavily slumped—in fact, almost entirely subsided—after its first short-lived boom. One or two important books on the subject appeared—Steinmetz's inquiries into the beginnings of punishment, Durkheim's analysis of early criminal and civil law— but, on the whole, the first impetus has proved so little inspiring that most modern anthropologists, both in theory and in field-work, ignore its very existence. In the standard manual *Notes and Queries on Anthropology*, 'law' appears neither in the index nor in the table of contents, and the few lines devoted to it under the heading of "Government : Politics", excellent as they are, do not correspond in any way to the importance of the subject. In the book of the late Dr. Rivers on *Social Organization* the problem of primitive law is discussed only incidentally, and, as we shall see, it is rather banished from primitive sociology than included in it by the author's brief reference.

This lacuna in modern anthropology is due, not to any oversight of primitive legality, but on the contrary to its over-emphasis. Paradoxical as it sounds, it is yet true that present-day anthropology neglects primitive law just because it has an exaggerated, and I will add at once, a mistaken idea of its perfection.

B

PART I

PRIMITIVE LAW AND ORDER

I

THE AUTOMATIC SUBMISSION TO CUSTOM
AND THE REAL PROBLEM

WHEN we come to inquire why rules of conduct, however hard, irksome, or unwelcome, are obeyed; what makes private life, economic co-operation, public events run so smoothly; of what, in short, consist the forces of law and order in savagery—the answer is not easy to give, and what anthropology has had to say about it is far from satisfactory. So long as it could be maintained that the ' savage ' is really savage, that he follows what little law he has but fitfully and loosely, the problem did not exist. When the question became actual, when it became plain that hypertrophy of rules rather than lawlessness is characteristic of primitive life, scientific opinion veered round to the opposite point: the savage was made not only into a model of the law-abiding citizen, but it became an axiom that in submitting to all his tribal rules and fetters, he follows the natural trend of his spontaneous impulses; that in this way he glides, so to speak, along the line of least resistance.

The savage—so runs to-day's verdict of competent

anthropologists—has a deep reverence for tradition and custom, an automatic submission to their biddings. He obeys them 'slavishly', 'unwittingly', 'spontaneously', through 'mental inertia', combined with the fear of public opinion or of supernatural punishment; or again through a 'pervading group-sentiment if not group-instinct'. Thus we find the following in a recent book: "The savage is far from being the free and unfettered creature of Rousseau's imagination. On the contrary, he is hemmed in on every side by the customs of his people, he is bound in the chains of immemorial tradition not merely in his social relations, but in his religion, his medicine, in his industry, his art: in short, every aspect of his life" (E. Sidney Hartland in *Primitive Law*, p. 138). With all this we might agree, except that it seems doubtful whether the "chains of tradition" are identical or even similar in art and in social relations, in industry, and in religion. But when, immediately, we are told that "these fetters are accepted by him (the savage) as a matter of course; he never seeks to break forth"—we must enter a protest. Is it not contrary to human nature to accept any constraint as a matter of course, and does man, whether civilized or savage, ever carry out unpleasant, burdensome, cruel regulations and taboos without being compelled to? And compelled by some force or motive which he cannot resist?

Yet this automatic acquiescence, this instinctive submission of every member of the tribe to its laws, is the fundamental axiom laid at the basis of the inquiry into primitive order and adherence to rule. Thus another foremost authority on the subject, the late Dr. Rivers, speaks in the book already mentioned of an " unwitting or intuitive method of regulating social life ", which is, according to him, " closely connected with primitive communism." And he proceeds to tell us : " Among such a people as the Melanesians there is a group sentiment which makes unnecessary any definite social machinery for the exertion of authority, in just the same manner as it makes possible the harmonious working of communal ownership, and insures the peaceful character of a communistic system of sexual relations " (*Social Organization*, p. 169).

Thus here again we are assured that ' unwitting ' or ' intuitive methods ', ' instinctive submission ' and some mysterious ' group-sentiment ' account for law, order, communism and sexual promiscuity alike ! This sounds altogether like a Bolshevik paradise, but is certainly not correct in reference to Melanesian societies, which I know at first hand.

A similar idea is expressed by a third writer, a sociologist, who has contributed more towards our understanding of the organization of savages from the point of view of mental and social evolution than perhaps any one living anthropologist. Professor

Hobhouse, speaking of the tribes on a very low level of culture, affirms that " such societies, of course, have their customs, which are doubtless felt as binding by their members, but if we mean by law a body of rules enforced by an authority independent of personal ties of kinship and friendship, such an institution is not compatible with their social organization " (*Morals in Evolution*, 1915, p. 73). Here we have to question the phrase " felt as binding " and ask whether it does not cover and hide the real problem instead of solving it. Is there not, with regard to some rules at least, a binding mechanism, not perhaps enforced by any central authority, but backed up by real motives, interests and complex sentiments ? Can severe prohibitions, onerous duties, very burdensome and galling liabilities, be made binding by a mere ' feeling ' ? We should like to know more about this invaluable mental attitude, but the author simply takes it for granted. Again, the minimum definition of law as the " body of rules enforced by an authority independent of personal ties ", seems to me to be too narrow and not to lay the emphasis on the relevant elements. There are among the many norms of conduct in savage societies certain rules regarded as compulsory obligations of one individual or group towards another individual or group. The fulfilment of such obligations is usually rewarded according to the measure of its perfection, while non-compliance is

visited upon the remiss agent. Taking our stand upon
such a comprehensive view of law and inquiring
into the nature of the forces which make it obligatory,
we shall be able to arrive at much more satisfactory
results than if we were to discuss questions of authority,
government and punishment.

To take another representative opinion, that of one
of the highest anthropological authorities in the United
States, we find Dr. Lowie expressing a very similar
view : " Generally speaking, the unwritten laws of
customary usage are obeyed far more willingly than
our written codes, or rather they are obeyed
spontaneously." [1] To compare the ' willingness ' in
obedience to law of an Australian savage with a New
Yorker, or of a Melanesian with a nonconformist
citizen of Glasgow, is a perilous proceeding and its
results have to be taken very ' generally ' indeed,
until they lose all meaning. The fact is that no society
can work in an efficient manner unless laws are obeyed
' willingly ' and ' spontaneously '.   The threat of
coercion and the fear of punishment do not touch the
average man, whether ' savage ' or ' civilized ', while,
on the other hand, they are indispensable with regard
to certain turbulent or criminal elements in either
society. Again, there is a number of laws, taboos and
obligations in every human culture which weigh heavily
on every citizen, demand great self-sacrifice, and are

[1] *Primitive Society*, Chap. on " Justice ", p. 387, English edition.

obeyed for moral, sentimental or matter-of-fact reasons, but without any ' spontaneity '.

It would be easy to multiply statements and to show that the dogma of the automatic submission to custom dominates the whole inquiry into primitive law. In all fairness, however, it must be stressed that any shortcomings in theory or observation are due to the real difficulties and pitfalls of which this subject is so full.

The extreme difficulty of the problem lies, I think, in the very complex and diffuse nature of the forces which constitute primitive law.   Accustomed as we are to look for a definite machinery of enactment, administration, and enforcement of law, we cast round for something analogous in a savage community and, failing to find there any similar arrangements, we conclude that all law is obeyed by this mysterious propensity of the savage to obey it.

Anthropology seems here to be faced by a similar difficulty as the one overcome by Tylor in his " minimum definition of religion ". By defining the forces of law in terms of central authority, codes, courts, and constables, we must come to the conclusion that law needs no enforcement in a primitive community and is followed spontaneously. That the savage does break the law sometimes, though rarely and occasionally, has been recorded by observers and taken into account by builders of anthropological theory, who have always maintained that criminal law is the only law of savages. But that his observance of the rules of law under the normal conditions, when it is followed and not defied, is at best partial, conditional, and subject to evasions; that it is not enforced by any wholesale motive like fear of punishment, or a general submission to all tradition, but by very complex psychological and social inducements—all this is a state of affairs which modern anthropology has so far completely overlooked. In the following account I shall try to establish it for one ethnographic province, north-west Melanesia, and I shall show reasons why observations of similar nature to those carried out by myself should be extended to other societies in order to give us some idea about their legal conditions.

We shall approach our facts with a very elastic and wide conception of the problem before us. In looking for 'law' and legal forces, we shall try merely to discover and analyse all the rules conceived and acted upon as binding obligations, to find out the nature of the binding forces, and to classify the rules according to the manner in which they are made valid. We shall see that by an inductive examination of facts, carried out without any preconceived idea or ready-made definition, we shall be enabled to arrive at a satisfactory classification of the norms and rules of a primitive community, at a clear distinction of primitive law from other forms of custom, and at a new, dynamic

conception of the social organization of savages. Since
the facts of primitive law described in this article have
been recorded in Melanesia, the classical area of
' communism ' and ' promiscuity ', of ' group-
sentiment ', ' clan-solidarity ', and ' spontaneous
obedience ', the conclusions we shall be able
to draw—which will dispose of these catch-words
and all they stand for—may be of special interest.

II

MELANESIAN ECONOMICS AND THE THEORY OF PRIMITIVE COMMUNISM

THE Trobriand Archipelago, which is inhabited by the Melanesian community referred to, lies to the north-east of New Guinea and consists of a group of flat coral islands, surrounding a wide lagoon. The plains of the land are covered with fertile soil and the lagoon teems with fish, while both afford easy means of inter-communication to the inhabitants. Accordingly, the islands support a dense population mainly engaged in agriculture and fishing, but expert also in various arts and crafts and keen on trade and exchange.

Like all coral islanders, they spend a great deal of their time on the central lagoon. On a calm day it is alive with canoes carrying people or produce, or engaged in one of their manifold systems of fishing. A superficial acquaintance with these pursuits might leave one with an impression of arbitrary disorder, anarchy, complete lack of system. Patient and painstaking observations would soon reveal, however, not only that the natives have definite technical systems of catching fish and complex economic arrangements, but also that they have a close organization in their working teams, and a fixed division of social functions.

Thus, within each canoe it would be found that there is one man who is its rightful owner, while the rest act as a crew. All these men, who as a rule belong to the same sub-clan, are bound to each other and to their fellow-villagers by mutual obligations; when the whole community go out fishing, the owner cannot refuse his canoe. He must go out himself or let some one else do it instead. The crew are equally under an obligation to him. For reasons which will presently become clear, each man must fill his place and stand by his task. Each man also receives his fair share in the distribution of the catch as an equivalent of his service. Thus the ownership and use of the canoe consist of a series of definite obligations and duties uniting a group of people into a working team.

What makes the conditions even more complex is that the owners and the members of the crew are entitled to surrender their privileges to any one of their relatives and friends. This is often done, but always for a consideration, for a repayment. To an observer who does not grasp all the details, and does not follow all the intricacies of each transaction, such a state of affairs looks very much like communism: the canoe appears to be owned jointly by a group and used indiscriminately by the whole community.

Dr. Rivers in fact tells us that " one of the objects of

Melanesian culture which is usually, if not always, the subject of common ownership is the canoe ", and further on, in reference to this statement, he speaks about " the great extent to which communistic sentiments concerning property dominate the people of Melanesia " (*Social Organization*, pp. 106 and 107). In another work, the same writer speaks about " the socialistic or even communistic behaviour of such societies as those of Melanesia " (*Psychology and Politics*, pp. 86 and 87). Nothing could be more mistaken than such generalizations. There is a strict distinction and definition in the rights of every one and this makes ownership anything but communistic. We have in Melanesia a compound and complex system of holding property, which in no way partakes of the nature of ' socialism ' or ' communism '. A modern joint-stock company might just as well be called a ' communistic enterprise '. As a matter of fact, any descriptions of a savage institution in terms such as 'communism', 'capitalism' or 'joint-stock company', borrowed from present-day economic conditions or political controversy, cannot but be misleading.

The only correct proceeding is to describe the legal state of affairs in terms of concrete fact. Thus, the ownership of a Trobriand fishing canoe is defined by the manner in which the object is made, used and regarded by the group of men who produced it and enjoy its possession. The master of the canoe, who acts at the same time as the head of the team and as the fishing magician of the canoe, has first of all to finance the building of a new craft, when the old one is worn out, and he has to maintain it in good repair, helped in this by the rest of his crew. In this they remain under mutual obligations to one another to appear each at his post, while every canoe is bound to come when a communal fishing has been arranged.

In using the craft, every joint owner has a right to a certain place in it and to certain duties, privileges, and benefits associated with it. He has his post in the canoe, he has his task to perform, and enjoys the corresponding title, either of ' master ' or ' steersman ', or ' keeper of the nets ', or ' watcher for fish '. His position and title are determined by the combined action of rank, age, and personal ability. Each canoe also has its place in the fleet and its part to play in the manœuvres of joint fishing. Thus on a close inquiry we discover in this pursuit a definite system of division of functions and a rigid system of mutual obligations, into which a sense of duty and the recognition of the need of co-operation enter side by side with a realization of self-interest, privileges and benefits. Ownership, therefore, can be defined neither by such words as ' communism ' nor ' individualism ', nor by reference to ' joint-stock company ' system or ' personal enterprise ', but by the concrete facts and conditions of use. It is the sum of duties, privileges and mutualities which bind the joint owners to the object and to each other.

Thus, in connexion with the first object which attracted our attention—the native canoe—we are met by law, order, definite privileges and a well-developed system of obligations.

III

THE BINDING FORCE OF ECONOMIC OBLIGATIONS

TO enter more deeply into the nature of these binding obligations, let us follow the fishermen to the shore. Let us see what happens with the division of the catch. In most cases only a small proportion of it remains with the villagers. As a rule we should find a number of people from some inland community waiting on the shore. They receive the bundles of fish from the fishermen and carry them home, often many miles away, running so as to arrive while it is still fresh. Here again we should find a system of mutual services and obligations based on a standing arrangement between two village communities. The inland village supplies the fishermen with vegetables : the coastal community repays with fish. This arrangement is primarily an economic one. It has also a ceremonial aspect, for the exchange has to be done according to an elaborate ritual. But there is also the legal side, a system of mutual obligations which forces the fisherman to repay whenever he has received a gift from his inland partner, and vice versa. Neither partner can refuse, neither may stint in his return gift, neither should delay.

PLATE II.

Bundles of Fish taken over from the Fishermen by the Inland Natives.

[*face* page 22.]

What is the motive force behind these obligations ? The coastal and inland villages respectively have to reply upon each other for the supply of food. On the coast the natives never have enough vegetable food, while inland the people are always in need of fish. Moreover, custom will have it that on the coast all the big ceremonial displays and distributions of food, which form an extremely important aspect of the public life of these natives, must be made with certain specially large and fine varieties of vegetable food, which grow only on the fertile plains inland. There, on the other hand, the proper substance for a distribution and feast is fish. Thus to all other reasons of value of the respectively rarer food, there is added an artificially, culturally created dependence of the two districts upon one another. So that on the whole each community is very much in need of its partners. If at any time previously these have been guilty of neglect, however, they know that they will be in one way or another severely penalized. Each community has, therefore, a weapon for the enforcement of its rights : reciprocity.

This is not limited to the exchange of fish for vegetables. As a rule, two communities rely upon each other in other forms of trading and other mutual services as well. Thus every chain of reciprocity is made the more binding by being part and parcel of a whole system of mutualities.

IV

RECIPROCITY AND DUAL ORGANIZATION

I HAVE found only one writer who fully appreciates the importance of reciprocity in primitive social organization. The leading German anthropologist, Prof. Thurnwald of Berlin, clearly recognizes " die Symmetrie des Gesellschaftsbaus " and the corresponding " Symmetrie von Handlungen ".[1] Throughout his monograph, which is perhaps the best account of the social organization of a savage tribe extant, Prof. Thurnwald shows how the symmetry of social structure and of actions pervades native life. Its importance as a legal binding form is not, however, explicitly stated by the writer, who seems to be aware of its psychological foundation ' in human feeling ' rather than of its social function in safeguarding the continuity and adequacy of mutual services.

The old theories of tribal dichotomy, the discussions about the ' origins ' of ' phratries ' or ' moieties ' and

---

[1] "Die Symmetrie von Handlungen aber nennen wir das Prinzip der Vergeltung. Dieses liegt tief verwurzelt im menschlichen Empfinden—als adaquate Reaktion—und ihm kam von jeher die grösste Bedeutung im sozialen Leben zu " (*Die Gemeinde der Bánaro*, Stuttgart, 1921, p. 10).

of the duality in tribal subdivisions, never entered into
the inner or differential foundations of the external
phenomenon of halving. The recent treatment of the
' dual organization ' by the late Dr. Rivers and his
school suffers badly from the defect of looking for
recondite causes instead of analysing the phenomenon
itself.   The dual principle is neither the result of
' fusion ' nor ' splitting ' nor of any other sociological
cataclysm. It is the integral result of the inner
symmetry of all social transactions, of the reciprocity
of services, without which no primitive community
could exist.   A dual organization may appear clearly
in the division of a tribe into two ' moieties ' or
be almost completely obliterated—but I venture to
foretell that wherever careful inquiry be made,
symmetry of structure will be found in every savage
society, as the indispensable basis of reciprocal
obligations.

The sociological manner in which the relations of
reciprocity are arranged, makes them yet more
stringent. Between the two communities the exchanges
are not carried out haphazard, any two individuals
trading with each other at random. On the contrary,
every man has his permanent partner in the exchange,
and the two have to deal with each other. They are
often relatives-in-law, or else sworn friends, or partners
in the important system of ceremonial exchange called
kula. Within each community again the individual

partners are ranged into totemic sub-clans. So that the exchange establishes a system of sociological ties of an economic nature, often combined with other ties between individual and individual, kinship group and kinship group, village and village, district and district.

Going over the relations and transactions previously described, it is easy to see that the same principle of mutuality supplies the sanction for each rule. There is in every act a sociological dualism : two parties who exchange services and functions, each watching over the measure of fulfilment and the fairness of conduct of the other.   The master of the canoe, whose interests and ambitions are bound up with his craft, looks after order in the internal transactions between the members of the crew and represents the latter externally.   To him each member of the crew is bound at the time of construction and ever after, when co-operation is necessary. Reciprocally, the master has to give each man the ceremonial payment at the feast of construction ; the master cannot refuse any one his place in the boat ; and he has to see that each man receives his fair share of the catch.   In this and in all the manifold activities of economic order, the social behaviour of the natives is based on a well-assessed give-and-take, always mentally ticked off and in the long run balanced.   There is no wholesale discharge of duties or acceptance of privileges ; no ' communistic ' disregard of tally and ear-mark.   The free and easy way in which all transactions are done, the good manners which pervade all and cover any hitches or maladjustments, make it difficult for the superficial observer to see the keen self-interest and watchful reckoning which runs right through. To one who knows the natives intimately, nothing is more patent than this. The same control which the master assumes within his canoe, is taken within the community by the headman who is, as a rule, also the hereditary magician.

V

LAW, SELF-INTEREST, AND SOCIAL AMBITION

IT scarcely needs to be added that there are also other driving motives, besides the constraint of reciprocal obligations, which keep the fishermen to their task. The utility of the pursuit, the craving for the fresh, excellent diet, above all, perhaps, the attraction of what to the natives is an intensely fascinating sport—move them more obviously, more consciously even, and more effectively than what we have described as the legal obligation. But the social constraint, the regard for the effective rights and claims of others is always prominent in the mind of the natives as well as in their behaviour, once this is well understood. It is also indispensable to ensure the smooth working of their institutions. For in spite of all zest and attractions, there are on each occasion a few individuals, indisposed, moody, obsessed by some other interest—very often by an intrigue—who would like to escape from their obligation, if they could. Anyone who knows how extremely difficult, if not impossible, it is to organize a body of Melanesians for even a short and amusing pursuit requiring concerted action, and how well and readily they set to work in their customary enterprises, will realize the function and the need of compulsion, due to the native's conviction that another man has a claim on his work.

There is yet another force which makes the obligations still more binding. I have mentioned already the ceremonial aspect of the transactions. The gifts of food in the system of exchange described above must be offered according to strict formalities, in specially made measures of wood, carried and presented in a prescribed manner, in a ceremonial procession and with a blast of conch-shells. Now nothing has a greater sway over the Melanesian's mind than ambition and vanity associated with a display of food and wealth. In the giving of gifts, in the distribution of their surplus, they feel a manifestation of power, and an enhancement of personality. The Trobriander keeps his food in houses better made and more highly ornamented than his dwelling huts. Generosity is the highest virtue to him, and wealth the essential element of influence and rank. The association of a semi-commercial transaction with definite public ceremonies supplies another binding force of fulfilment through a special psychological mechanism: the desire for display, the ambition to appear munificent, the extreme esteem for wealth and for the accumulation of food.

We have thus gained some insight into the nature of the mental and social forces which make certain rules

of conduct into binding law. Nor is the binding force
superfluous.   Whenever the native can evade his
obligations without the loss of prestige, or without the
prospective loss of gain, he does so, exactly as a
civilized business man would do. When the ' automatic
smoothness ' in the run of obligations so often
attributed to the Melanesian is studied more closely,
it becomes clear that there are constant hitches in the
transactions, that there is much grumbling and
recrimination and seldom is a man completely satisfied
with his partner. But, on the whole, he continues in
the partnership and, on the whole, every one tries to
fulfil his obligations, for he is impelled to do so partly
through enlightened self-interest, partly in obedience
to his social ambitions and sentiments. Take the real
savage, keen on evading his duties, swaggering and
boastful when he has fulfilled them, and compare him
with the anthropologist's dummy who slavishly follows
custom and automatically obeys every regulation.
There is not the remotest resemblance between the
teachings of anthropology on this subject and the
reality of native life. We begin to see how the dogma
of mechanical obedience to law would prevent the
field-worker from seeing the really relevant facts of
primitive legal organization. We understand now that
the rules of law, the rules with a definite binding
obligation, stand out from the mere rules of custom.
We can see also that civil law, consisting of positive

ordinances, is much more developed than the body of mere prohibitions, and that a study of purely criminal law among savages misses the most important phenomena of their legal life.

It is also obvious that the type of rules which we have been discussing, although they are unquestionably rules of binding law, have in no way the character of religious commandments, laid down absolutely, obeyed rigidly and integrally. The rules here described are essentially elastic and adjustable, leaving a considerable latitude within which their fulfilment is regarded as satisfactory. The bundles of fish, the measures of yams, or bunches of taro, can only be roughly assessed, and naturally the quantities exchanged vary according to whether the fishing season or the harvest is more abundant. All this is taken into account and only wilful stinginess, neglect, or laziness are regarded as a breach of contract. Since, again, largesse is a matter of honour and praise, the average native will strain all his resources to be lavish in his measure. He knows, moreover, that any excess in zeal and generosity is bound sooner or later to be rewarded.

We can see now that a narrow and rigid conception of the problem—a definition of ' law ' as the machinery of carrying out justice in cases of trespass — would leave on one side all the phenomena to which we have referred. In all the facts described, the element or aspect of law, that is of effective social constraint, consists in the complex arrangements which make people keep to their obligations. Among them the most important is the manner in which many transactions are linked into chains of mutual services, every one of them having to be repaid at some later date. The public and ceremonial manner in which these transactions are usually carried out, combined with the great ambition and vanity of the Melanesian adds also to the safe-guarding forces of law.

VI

THE RULES OF LAW IN RELIGIOUS ACTS

I HAVE referred so far mainly to economic relations, for civil law is primarily concerned with owner- ship and wealth among savages as well as among ourselves. But we could find the legal aspect in any other domain of tribal life. Take for example the most characteristic acts of ceremonial life—the rites of mourning and sorrow for the dead. At first we perceive in them, naturally, their religious character : they are acts of piety towards the deceased, caused by fear or love or solicitude for the spirit of the departed. As the ritual and public display of emotion they are also part of the ceremonial life of the community.

Who, however, would suspect a legal side to such religious transactions ? Yet in the Trobriands there is not one single mortuary act, not one ceremony, which is not considered to be an obligation of the performer towards some of the other survivors. The widow weeps and wails in ceremonial sorrow, in religious piety and fear—but also because the strength of her grief affords direct satisfaction to the deceased man's brothers and maternal relatives. It is the matrilineal group of

kindred who, according to the native theory of kinship
and mourning, are the people really bereaved.   The
wife, though she lived with her husband, though she
should grieve at his death, though often she really and
sincerely does so, remains but a stranger by the rules
of matrilineal kinship.   It is her duty towards the
surviving members of her husband's clan, accordingly,
to display her grief, to keep a long period of mourning
and to carry the jaw-bone of her husband for some
years after his death.   Nor is this obligation without
reciprocity.   At the first big ceremonial distribution,
some three days after her husband's death, she will
receive from his kinsmen a ritual payment, and a
substantial one, for her tears ; and at later ceremonial
feasts she is given more payments for the subsequent
services of mourning.   It should also be kept in mind
that to the natives mourning is but a link in the life-
long chain of reciprocities between husband and wife
and between their respective families.

PLATE III.

Obligatory display of grief in Ritual Wailing.

[*face* page 34.]

VII

THE LAW OF MARRIAGE

THIS brings us to the subject of marriage, extremely
important for the understanding of native law.
Marriage establishes not merely a bond between
husband and wife, but it also imposes a standing
relation of mutuality between the man and the wife's
family, especially her brother. A woman and her
brother are bound to each other by characteristic and
highly important ties of kinship. In a Trobriand
family a female must always remain under the special
guardianship of one man—one of her brothers, or, if
she has none, her nearest maternal kinsman. She has
to obey him and to fulfil a number of duties, while he
looks after her welfare and provides for her economically
even after she is married.

The brother becomes the natural warden of her
children, who therefore have to regard him and not
their father as the legal head of the family. He in
turn has to look after them, and to supply the
household with a considerable proportion of its food.
This is the more burdensome since marriage being

patrilocal, the girl has moved away to her husband's community, so that every time at harvest there is a general economic *chassé-croisé* all over the district.

After the crops are taken out, the yams are classified and the pick of the crop from each garden is put into a conical heap. The main heap in each garden plot is always for the sister's household. The sole purpose of all the skill and labour devoted to this display of food is the satisfaction of the gardener's ambition. The whole community, nay, the whole district, will see the garden produce, comment upon it, criticize, or praise. A big heap proclaims, in the words of my informant : " Look what I have done for my sister and her family. I am a good gardener and my nearest relatives, my sister and her children, will never suffer for want of food." After a few days the heap is dismantled, the yams carried in baskets to the sister's village, where they are put up into exactly the same shape in front of the yam-house of the sister's husband ; there again the members of the community will see the heap and admire it. This whole ceremonial side of the transaction has a binding force which we know already. The display, the comparisons, the public assessment impose a definite psychological constraint upon the giver— they satisfy and reward him, when successful work enables him to give a generous gift, and they penalize and humiliate him for inefficiency, stinginess, or bad luck.

Besides ambition, reciprocity prevails in this transaction as everywhere else ; at times, indeed, it steps in almost upon the heels of an act of fulfilment. First of all the husband has to repay by definite periodical gifts every annual harvest contribution. Later on, when the children grow up, they will come directly under the authority of their maternal uncle ; the boys will have to help him, to assist him in everything, to contribute a definite quota to all the payments he has to make. His sister's daughters do but little for him directly, but indirectly, in a matrilineal society, they provide him with his heirs and descendants of two generations below.

Thus placing the harvest offerings within their sociological context, and taking a long view of the relationship, we see that every one of its transactions is justified as a link in the chain of mutualities. Yet taking it isolated, torn out of its setting, each transaction appears nonsensical, intolerably burdensome and sociologically meaningless, also no doubt ' communistic ' ! What could be more economically absurd than this oblique distribution of garden produce, where every man works for his sister and has to rely in turn on his wife's brother, where more time and energy is apparently wasted on display, on show, on the shifting of the goods, than on real work ? Yet a closer analysis shows that some of these apparently unnecessary actions are powerful economic incentives,

D

that others supply the legal binding force, while others, again, are the direct result of native kinship ideas. It is also clear that we can understand the legal aspect of such relations only if we look upon them integrally without over-emphasizing any one link in the chain of reciprocal duties.

VIII

THE PRINCIPLE OF GIVE AND TAKE PERVADING TRIBAL LIFE

IN the foregoing we have seen a series of pictures
from native life, illustrating the legal aspect of the
marriage relationship, of co-operation in a fishing
team, of food barter between inland and coastal
villages, of certain ceremonial duties of mourning.
These examples were adduced with some detail, in
order to bring out clearly the concrete working of
what appears to me to be the real mechanism of law,
social and psychological constraint, the actual forces,
motives, and reasons which make men keep to their
obligations. If space permitted it would be easy to
bring these isolated instances into a coherent picture
and to show that in all social relations and in all the
various domains of tribal life, exactly the same legal
mechanism can be traced, that it places the *binding
obligations* in a special category and sets them apart
from other types of customary rules. A rapid though
comprehensive survey will have to suffice.

To take the economic transactions first : barter
of goods and services is carried on mostly within a

standing partnership, or is associated with definite social ties or coupled with a mutuality in non-economic matters. Most if not all economic acts are found to belong to some chain of reciprocal gifts and counter-gifts, which in the long run balance, benefiting both sides equally.

I have already given an account of the economic conditions in N.W. Melanesia, in " The Primitive Economics of the Trobriand Islanders " (*Economic Journal*, 1921) and in *Argonauts of the Western Pacific*, 1923. Chapter vi of that volume deals with matters here discussed, i.e. the forms of economic exchange. My ideas about primitive law were not mature at that time, and the facts are presented there without any reference to the present argument—their testimony only the more telling because of that. When, however, I describe a category of offerings as ' Pure Gifts ' and place under this heading the gifts of husband to wife and of father to children, I am obviously committing a mistake. I have fallen then, in fact, into the error exposed above, of tearing the act out of its context, of not taking a sufficiently long view of the chain of transactions. In the same paragraph I have supplied, however, an implicit rectification of my mistake in stating that " a gift given by the father to his son is said [by the natives] to be a repayment for the man's relationship to the mother " (p. 179). I have also pointed out there that the ' free gifts ' to the wife are also based on the same idea. But the really correct account of the conditions—correct both from the legal and from the economic point of view—would have been to embrace the whole system of gifts, duties, and mutual benefits exchanged between the husband on one hand, wife, children, and wife's brother on the other. It would be found then in native ideas that the system is based on a very complex give and take, and that in the long run the mutual services balance.[1]

The real reason why all these economic obligations are normally kept, and kept very scrupulously, is that failure to comply places a man in an intolerable position, while slackness in fulfilment covers him with opprobrium. The man who would persistently disobey the rulings of law in his economic dealings would soon find himself outside the social and economic order—and he is perfectly well aware of it. Test cases are supplied nowadays, when a number of natives through laziness, eccentricity, or a non-conforming spirit of enterprise, have chosen to ignore the obligations of

---

[1] Compare also the apposite criticism of my expression " pure gift " and of all it implies by M. Marcel Mauss, in *L'Année Sociologique*, Nouvelle Série, vol. i, pp. 171 sqq. I had written the above paragraph before I saw M. Mauss's strictures, which substantially agreed with my own. It is gratifying to a field-worker when his observations are sufficiently well presented to allow others to refute his conclusions out of his own material. It is even more pleasant for me to find that my maturer judgment has led me independently to the same results as those of my distinguished friend M. Mauss.

their status and have become automatically outcasts and hangers-on to some white man or other.

The honourable citizen is bound to carry out his duties, though his submission is not due to any instinct or intuitive impulse or mysterious ' group-sentiment ', but to the detailed and elaborate working of a system, in which every act has its own place and must be performed without fail. Though no native, however intelligent, can formulate this state of affairs in a general abstract manner, or present it as a sociological theory, yet every one is well aware of its existence and in each concrete case he can foresee the consequences.

In magical and religious ceremonies almost every act, besides its primary purposes and effects, is also regarded as an obligation between groups and individuals, and here also there comes sooner or later an equivalent repayment or counter-service, stipulated by custom. Magic in its most important forms is a public institution in which the communal magician, who as a rule holds his office by inheritance, has to officiate on behalf of the whole group. Such is the case in the magic of gardens, fishing, war, weather, and canoe-building. As necessity arises, at the proper season, or in certain circumstances he is under an obligation to perform his magic, to keep the taboos, and at times also to control the whole enterprise. For this he is repaid by small offerings, immediately given, and often incorporated into the ritual proceedings. But the real reward lies in the prestige, power, and privileges which his position confers upon him.[1]   In cases of minor or occasional magic, such as love charms, curative rites, sorcery, magic of toothache and of pig-welfare, when it is performed on behalf of another, it has to be paid for substantially and the relation between client and professional is based on a contract defined by custom. From the point of view of our present argument, we have to register the fact that all the acts of communal magic are obligatory upon the performer, and that the obligation to carry them out goes with the status of communal magician, which is hereditary in most cases and always is a position of power and privilege. A man may relinquish his position and hand it over to the next in succession, but once he accepts it, he has to carry on the work incumbent, and the community has to give him in return all his dues.

As to the acts which usually would be regarded as religious rather than magical—ceremonies at birth or marriage, rites of death and mourning, the worship of ghosts, spirits, or mythical personages—they also have a legal side clearly exemplified in the case of mortuary performances, described above.   Every

[1] For further data referring to the social and legal status of the hereditary magician, see Chap. xvii on " Magic ", in *Argonauts of the Western Pacific*, as well as the descriptions of and sundry references to canoe magic, sailing magic, and *kaloma* magic. Compare also the short account of garden magic in " Primitive Economics " (*Economic Journ.*, 1921) ;   of war magic, in *Man*, 1920 (No. 5 of article) ;   and of fishing magic, in *Man*, 1918 (No. 53 of article).

important act of a religious nature is conceived as a moral obligation towards the object, the ghost, spirit, or power worshipped ; it also satisfies some emotional craving of the performer ; but besides all this it has also as a matter of fact its place in some social scheme, it is regarded by some third person or persons as due to them, watched and then repaid or returned in kind. When, for example, at the annual return of the departed ghosts to their village you give an offering to the spirit of a dead relative, you satisfy his feelings, and no doubt also his spiritual appetite, which feeds on the spiritual substance of the meal ; you probably also express your own sentiment towards the beloved dead. But there is also a social obligation involved : after the dishes have been exposed for some time and the spirit has finished with his spiritual share, the rest, none the worse it appears for ordinary consumption after its spiritual abstraction, is given to a friend or relation-in-law still alive, who then returns a similar gift later on.[1] I can recall to my mind not one single act of a religious nature without some such sociological by-play more or less directly associated with the main religious function of the act. Its importance lies in the fact that it makes the act a social obligation, besides its being a religious duty.

[1] Comp. the writer's account of the *Milamala*, the feast of the annual return of the spirits, in " Baloma ; the spirits of the dead in the Trobriand Islands " (*Journ. of the R. Anthrop. Institute*, 1916). The food offerings in question are described on p. 378.

I could still continue with the survey of some other phases of tribal life and discuss more fully the legal aspect of domestic relations, already exemplified above, or enter into the reciprocities of the big enterprises, and so on. But it must have become clear now that the detailed illustrations previously given are not exceptional isolated cases, but representative instances of what obtains in every walk of native life.

IX

RECIPROCITY AS THE BASIS OF SOCIAL STRUCTURE

AGAIN, recasting our whole perspective and looking at matters from the sociological point of view, i.e. taking one feature of the constitution of the tribe after another, instead of surveying the various types of their tribal activities, it would be possible to show that the whole structure of Trobriand society is founded on the principle of *legal status*. By this I mean that the claims of chief over commoners, husband over wife, parent over child, and vice versa, are not exercised arbitrarily and one-sidedly, but according to definite rules, and arranged into well-balanced chains of reciprocal services.

Even the chief, whose position is hereditary, based on highly venerable mythological traditions, surrounded with semi-religious awe, enhanced by a princely ceremonial of distance, abasement, and stringent taboos, who has a great deal of power, wealth, and executive means, has to conform to strict norms and is bound by legal fetters. When he wants to declare war, organize an expedition, or celebrate a festivity, he must issue formal summons, publicly announce his will, deliberate with the notables, receive the tribute, services and assistance of his subjects in a ceremonial manner, and finally repay them according to a definite scale.[1] It is enough to mention here what has been previously said about the sociological status of marriage, of the relations between husband and wife, and of the status between relatives-in-law.[2] The whole division into totemic clans, into sub-clans of a local nature and into village communities, is characterized by a system of reciprocal services and duties, in which the groups play a game of give and take.

What perhaps is most remarkable in the legal nature of social relations is that reciprocity, the give-and-take principle, reigns supreme also within the clan, nay within the nearest group of kinsmen. As we have seen already, the relation between the maternal uncle and

[1] Comp. for more detail, the various aspects of chieftainship I have brought out in art. cit. " Primitive Economics ", op. cit. (*Argonauts*), and the articles on " War " and on " Spirits ", also referred to previously.

[2] Here again I must refer to some of my other publications, where these matters have been treated in detail, though not from the present point of view. See the three articles published in *Psyche* of October, 1923 (" The Psychology of Sex in Primitive Societies ") ; April, 1924 (" Psycho-Analysis and Anthropology ") ; and January, 1925 (" Complex and Myth in Mother-Right "), in which many aspects of sexual psychology, of the fundamental ideas and customs of kinship and relationship, have been described. The two latter articles appear uniform with this work in my *Sex and Repression in Savage Society* (1926).

his nephews, the relations between brothers, nay the most unselfish relation, that between a man and his sister, are all and one founded on mutuality and the repayment of services. It is just this group which has always been accused of ' primitive communism '. The clan is often described as the only legal person, the one body and entity, in primitive jurisprudence. " The unit is not the individual, but the kin. The individual is but part of the kin," are the words of Mr. Sidney Hartland. This is certainly true if we take into consideration that part of social life in which the kinship group—totemic clan, phratry, moiety, or class—plays the reciprocity game against co-ordinate groups. But what about the perfect unity within the clan ? Here we are offered the universal solution of the " pervading group-sentiment, if not group-instinct ", which is said to be specially rampant in the part of the world with which we are concerned, inhabited by " a people dominated by such a group-sentiment as actuates the Melanesian " (Rivers). This, we know, is quite a mistaken view. Within the nearest kinship group rivalries, dissensions, the keenest egotism flourish and dominate indeed the whole trend of kinship relations. To this point I shall have to return presently, for more facts and more definitely telling ones are necessary finally to explode this myth of kinship-communism, of the perfect solidarity within the group related by direct descent, a myth recently revived by

Dr. Rivers, and in some danger therefore of gaining general currency.

Having thus shown the range of facts to which our argument applies, having shown indeed that *law* covers the whole culture and the entire tribal constitution of these natives, let us formulate our conclusions in a coherent manner

X

THE RULES OF CUSTOM DEFINED AND CLASSIFIED

A T the beginning of Section I examples were given of current opinions which attribute to primitive man an automatic obedience to law. Now with this assumption there are associated certain more special propositions which are universally current in anthropology and yet fatal to the study of primitive jurisprudence.

First of all, if the rules of custom are obeyed by the savage through sheer inability to break them, then no definition can be given of law, no distinction can be drawn between the rules of law, morals, manners, and other usages. For the only way in which we can classify rules of conduct is by reference to the motives and sanctions by which they are enforced. So that with the assumption of an automatic obedience to all custom, anthropology has to give up any attempt at introducing into the facts order and classification, which is the first task of science.

We have seen already that Mr. Sidney Hartland regards the rules of art, medicine, social organization, industry, and what-not as hopelessly mixed up and

lumped together in all savage societies, both in the
native's own comprehension and in the reality of
social life. He states this view emphatically on several
occasions : " . . . The savage's perception of resemblances differs very much from our own. He
sees resemblances between objects which, to our eyes,
have not a single point in common " (*l.c.* p. 139). " For
the savage . . . the policy of a tribe is one and indi-
visible. . . . They [the savages] see nothing grotesque
or incongruous in publishing in the name of God a code
combining ritual, moral, agricultural, and medical with
what we understand as strictly juridical prescriptions.
. . . We may sever religion from magic, and magic
from medicine ; the members of the community draw
no such distinctions " (pp. 213, 214).

In all this Mr. Sidney Hartland gives lucid and
moderate expression to the current views about
" primitive prelogical mentality ", " confused savage
categories ", and the general shapelessness of early
culture. These views, however, cover but one side of
the case, express but a half-truth—as regards law, the
views here quoted are not correct. The savages have
a class of obligatory rules, not endowed with any
mystical character, not set forth in " the name of God ",
not enforced by any supernatural sanction but provided
with a purely social binding force.

If we designate the sum total of rules, conventions,
and patterns of behaviour as the body of custom, there

is no doubt that the native feels a strong respect for all
of them, has a tendency to do what others do, what
every one approves of, and, if not drawn or driven in
another direction by his appetites or interests, will
follow the biddings of custom rather than any other
course. The force of habit, the awe of traditional
command and a sentimental attachment to it, the
desire to satisfy public opinion—all combine to make
custom be obeyed for its own sake. In this the
' savages ' do not differ from the members of any self-
contained community with a limited horizon, whether
this be an Eastern European ghetto, an Oxford college,
or a Fundamentalist Middle West community. But
love of tradition, conformism and the sway of custom
account but to a very partial extent for obedience to
rules among dons, savages, peasants, or Junkers.

Limiting ourselves strictly to savages once more,
there are among the Trobrianders a number of traditional rules instructing the craftsman how to ply his
trade. The inert and uncritical way in which these
rules are obeyed is due to the general ' conformism of
savages ' as we might call it. But in the main these
rules are followed because their practical utility is
recognized by reason and testified by experience.
Again, other injunctions of how to behave in associating
with your friends, relatives, superiors, equals and so on,
are obeyed because any deviation from them makes
a man feel and look, in the eyes of others, ridiculous,

clumsy, socially uncouth. These are the precepts of good manners, very developed in Melanesia and most strictly adhered to. There are further rules laying down the proceedings at games, sports, entertainments and festivities, rules which are the soul and substance of the amusement or pursuit and are kept because it is felt and recognized that any failure to ' play the game ' spoils it—that is, when the game is really a game. In all this, it will be noted, there are no mental forces of inclination or of self-interest, or even inertia, which would run counter to any rule and make its fulfilment a burden. It is quite as easy to follow the rule as not, and once you embark upon a sporting or pleasurable pursuit, you really can enjoy it only if you obey all its rules whether of art, manners, or the game.

There are also norms pertaining to things sacred and important, the rules of magical rite, funerary pomp and such like. These are primarily backed up by supernatural sanctions and by the strong feeling that sacred matters must not be tampered with. By an equally strong moral force are maintained certain rules of personal conduct towards near relatives, members of the household and others towards whom strong sentiments of friendship, loyalty, or devotion are felt, which back up the dictates of the social code.

This brief catalogue is not an attempt at a classification, but is mainly meant to indicate clearly that,

E

besides the rules of law, there are several other types of
norm and traditional commandment which are backed
up by motives or forces, mainly psychological, in any
case entirely different from those which are characteristic of law in that community.   Thus, though in my
survey attention has naturally been mainly focussed on
the legal machinery, I was not intent on proving that all
social rules are legal, but on the contrary, I wanted to
show that the rules of law form but one well-defined
category within the body of custom.

XI

AN ANTHROPOLOGICAL DEFINITION OF LAW

THE rules of law stand out from the rest in that they are felt and regarded as the obligations of one person and the rightful claims of another. They are sanctioned not by a mere psychological motive, but by a definite social machinery of binding force, based, as we know, upon mutual dependence, and realized in the equivalent arrangement of reciprocal services, as well as in the combination of such claims into strands of multiple relationship. The ceremonial manner in which most transactions are carried out, which entails public control and criticism, adds still more to their binding force.

We may therefore finally dismiss the view that 'group-sentiment' or 'collective responsibility' is the only or even the main force which ensures adhesion to custom and which makes it binding or legal. *Esprit de corps*, solidarity, pride in one's community and clan exist undoubtedly among the Melanesians—no social order could be maintained without them in any culture high or low. I only want to enter a caution against such exaggerated views as those of Rivers, Sidney Hartland, Durkheim, and others, which would make this unselfish, impersonal, unlimited group-loyalty the corner-stone of all social order in primitive cultures. The savage is neither an extreme ' collectivist ' nor an intransigent ' individualist '—he is, like man in general, a mixture of both.

It results also from the account here given that primitive law does not consist exclusively or even chiefly of negative injunctions, nor is all savage law criminal law. And yet it is generally held that with the description of crime and punishment the subject of jurisprudence is exhausted as far as a savage community is concerned. As a matter of fact the dogma of automatic obedience, i.e. the absolute rigidity of the rules of custom implies an over-emphasis of criminal law in primitive communities and a corresponding denial of the possibility of civil law. Absolutely rigid rules cannot be stretched or adapted to life, they need not be enforced—but they can be broken. So much even the believers in a primitive super-legality must admit. Hence crime is the only legal problem to be studied in primitive communities, there is no civil law among savages, nor any civil jurisprudence for anthropology to work out. This view has dominated comparative studies of law from Sir Henry Maine to the most recent authorities, such as Prof. Hobhouse, Dr. Lowie, and Mr. Sidney Hartland. Thus we read in Mr. Hartland's book that in primitive societies " the core of legislation is a series of taboos ", and that

" almost all early codes consist of prohibitions "
(*Primitive Law*, p. 214). And again, " the general
belief in the certainty of supernatural punishment and
the alienation of the sympathy of one's fellows generate
an *atmosphere of terror* which is quite sufficient to
prevent a breach of tribal customs . . ." (p. 8—the
italics are mine). There is no such " atmosphere of
terror " unless perhaps in the case of a few very exceptional and sacred rules of ritual and religion, and on the
other hand the breach of tribal customs is prevented by
a special machinery, the study of which is the real
field of primitive jurisprudence.

In all this again Mr. Hartland is not alone. Steinmetz
in his learned and competent analysis of primitive
punishment insists on the criminal character of early
jurisprudence, on the mechanical, rigid, almost un-
directed and unintentional nature of the penalties inflicted and on their religious basis. His views are fully
endorsed by the great French sociologists Durkheim and
Mauss, who add besides one more clause: that responsibility, revenge, in fact all legal reactions are founded in
the psychology of the group and not of the individual.[1]
Even such acute and well-informed sociologists as Prof.
Hobhouse and Dr. Lowie, the latter acquainted at first
hand with savages, seem to follow the trend of the

[1] Steinmetz, *Ethnologische Studien zur ersten Entwickelung der
Strafe*, 1894 ; Durkheim in *L'Année Sociologique*, i. pp. 353 sqq. ;
Mauss in *Revue de l'Histoire des Religions*, 1897.

general bias in their otherwise excellent chapters on justice in primitive societies.

In our own province we have so far met with positive commandments only, the breach of which is penalized but not punished, and the machinery of which can by no procrustean methods be stretched beyond the line which separates *civil* from *criminal* law. If we have to provide the rules described in these articles with some modern, hence necessarily inappropriate label, —they must be called the body of ' civil law ' of the Trobriand Islanders.

' Civil law,' the positive law governing all the phases of tribal life, consists then of a body of binding obligations, regarded as a right by one party and acknowledged as a duty by the other, kept in force by a specific mechanism of reciprocity and publicity inherent in the structure of their society. These rules of civil law are elastic and possess a certain latitude. They offer not only penalties for failure, but also premiums for an overdose of fulfilment. Their stringency is ensured through the rational appreciation of cause and effect by the natives, combined with a number of social and personal sentiments such as ambition, vanity, pride, desire of self-enhancement by display, and also attachment, friendship, devotion and loyalty to the kin.

It scarcely needs to be added that ' law ' and ' legal phenomena ', as we have discovered, described and

PLATE IV.

Ceremonial Offering of Yams, carried in specially made wooden measures.
(*See* page 29)

[*face* page 58.]

defined them in a part of Melanesia, do not consist in any independent institutions. Law represents rather an aspect of their tribal life, one side of their structure, than any independent, self-contained social arrangements. Law dwells not in a special system of decrees, which foresee and define possible forms of non-fulfilment and provide appropriate barriers and remedies. Law is the specific result of the configuration of obligations, which makes it impossible for the native to shirk his responsibility without suffering for it in the future.

XII

SPECIFIC LEGAL ARRANGEMENTS

THE rare quarrels which occur at times take the form of an exchange of public expostulation (*yakala*) in which the two parties assisted by friends and relatives meet, harangue one another, hurl and hurl back recriminations. Such litigation allows people to give vent to their feelings and shows the trend of public opinion, and thus it may be of assistance in settling disputes. Sometimes it seems, however, only to harden the litigants. In no case is there any definite sentence pronounced by a third party, and agreement is but seldom reached then and there. The *yakala* therefore is a special legal arrangement, but of small importance and not really touching the heart of legal constraint.

Some other specific legal mechanisms may also be mentioned here. One of them is the *kaytapaku*, the magical protection of property by means of conditional curses. When a man owns coco or areca palms in distant spots, where it is impossible to keep watch over them, he attaches a palm leaf to the trunk of the tree, an indication that a formula has been uttered, which automatically would bring down ailment on the thief.

Another institution which has a legal side is the *kaytu-butabu*, a form of magic performed over all the coco-nut trees of a community to bring about their fertility, as a rule in view of an approaching feast. Such magic entails a strict prohibition to gather the nuts or to partake of coco-nut, even when imported. A similar institution is the *gwara*.[1] A pole is planted on the reef, and this places a taboo on any export of certain valuable objects, exchanged ceremonially in the *kula*, while their importation on the contrary is encouraged. This is a sort of moratorium, stopping all payments, without any interference with the receipts, which also aims at an accumulation of valuable objects before a big ceremonial distribution. Another important legal feature is a sort of ceremonial contract, called *kayasa*.[2] Here the leader of an expedition, the master of a feast, or the *entrepreneur* in an industrial venture gives a big ceremonial distribution. Those who participate in it and benefit by the bounty are under an obligation to assist the leader throughout the enterprise.

All these institutions, *kayasa*, *kaytapaku*, and *kaytu-butabu*, entail special binding ties. But even they are not exclusively *legal*. It would be a great

---

[1] Comp. the account of this institution in *Argonauts of the Western Pacific* (references in Index s.v. *Gwara*). Also descriptions in Prof. Seligman's " Melanesians ", and in the present writer's " The Natives of Mailu " (*Trans. R. Soc. of S. Australia*, vol. 39), of the *gola* or *gora* among the Western Papuo-Melanesians.

[2] *Argonauts*. See in Index s.v. *Kayasa*.

mistake to deal with the subject of law by a simple enumeration of these few arrangements, each of which subserves a special end and fulfils a very partial function. The main province of law is in the social mechanism, which is to be found at the bottom of all the real obligations and covers a very vast portion of their custom, though by no means all of it, as we know.

XIII

CONCLUSION AND FORECAST

I HAVE dealt here only with one province of Melanesia, and the conclusions arrived at have naturally a limited range. These conclusions, however, are based on facts observed by a new method and regarded from a new point of view, so that they might stimulate other observers to take up a similar line of study in other parts of the world.

Let us sum up the contrast between current views on the subject and the facts here presented. In modern anthropological jurisprudence, it is universally assumed that all custom is law to the savage and that he has no law but his custom. All custom again is obeyed automatically and rigidly by sheer inertia. There is no civil law or its equivalent in savage societies. The only relevant facts are the occasional breaches in defiance of custom—the crimes. There is no mechanism of enforcement of the primitive rules of conduct except the punishment of flagrant crime. Modern anthropology, therefore, ignores and sometimes even explicitly denies the existence of any social arrangements or of any psychological motives which make primitive man obey a certain class of custom for

purely social reasons. According to Mr. Hartland and
all the other authorities, religious sanctions, supernatural penalties, group responsibility and solidarity,
taboo and magic are the main elements of jurisprudence in savagery.

All these contentions are, as I have already indicated,
either directly mistaken or only partially true, or, at
least, they can be said to place the reality of native life
in a false perspective. Perhaps there is no further need
to argue that no man, however ' savage ' or ' primitive '
will *instinctively* act against his instincts, or *unwittingly*
obey a rule which he feels inclined cunningly to
evade or wilfully to defy ; or that he will not *spontaneously* act in a manner contrary to all his appetites
and inclinations. The fundamental function of law is
to curb certain natural propensities, to hem in and
control human instincts and to impose a non-spon-
taneous, compulsory behaviour—in other words, to
ensure a type of co-operation which is based on mutual
concessions and sacrifices for a common end. A new
force, different from the innate, spontaneous endow-
ment must be present to perform this task.

In order to make this negative criticism conclusive,
we have given a positive statement of a concrete case
to present the facts of primitive law as it really is,
and have shown in what the compulsory nature of
primitive legal rules consists.

The Melanesian of the region here treated has

unquestionably the greatest respect for his tribal custom and tradition as such. Thus much may be conceded to the old views at the outset. All the rules of his tribe, trivial or important, pleasant or irksome, moral or utilitarian, are regarded by him with reverence and felt to be obligatory. But the force of custom, the glamour of tradition, if it stood alone, would not be enough to counteract the temptations of appetite or lust or the dictates of self-interest. The mere sanction of tradition—the conformism and conservatism of the ' savage '—operates often and operates alone in enforcing manners, customary usage, private and public behaviour in all cases where some rules are necessary to establish the mechanism of common life and co-operation and to allow of orderly proceedings—but where there is no need to encroach on self-interest and inertia or to prod into unpleasant action or thwart innate propensities.

There are other rules, dictates and imperatives which require and possess their special type of sanction, besides the mere glamour of tradition. The natives in the part of Melanesia described have to conform, for example, to a very exacting type of religious ritual, especially at burial and in mourning. There are, again, imperatives of behaviour between relations. There exists finally the sanction of tribal punishment, due to a reaction in anger and indignation of the whole community. By this sanction human life, property, and,

last though not least, personal honour are safeguarded
in a Melanesian community, as well as such institutions
as chieftainship, exogamy, rank and marriage, which
play a paramount part in their tribal constitution.

Each class of rules just enumerated is distinguishable
from the rest by its sanctions and by its relation to the
social organization of the tribe and to its culture. They
do not form this amorphous mass of tribal usage or
' cake of custom ' of which we have been hearing so
much. The last category, the fundamental rules safe-
guarding life, property and personality form the class
which might be described as ' criminal law '—very
often over-emphasized by anthropologists and falsely
connected with the problem of ' government ' and
' central authority ' and invariably torn out of its
proper context of other legal rules. For—and here we
come at last to the most important point—there exists
a class of binding rules which control most aspects of
tribal life, which regulate personal relations between
kinsmen, clansmen and tribesmen, settle economic
relations, the exercise of power and of magic, the status
of husband and wife and of their respective families.
These are the rules of a Melanesian community which
correspond to our civil law.

There is no religious sanction to these rules, no fear,
superstitious or rational, enforces them, no tribal
punishment visits their breach, nor even the stigma of

public opinion or moral blame. The forces which make these rules binding we shall lay bare and find them not simple but clearly definable, not to be described by one word or one concept, but very real none the less. The binding forces of Melanesian civil law are to be found in the concatenation of the obligations, in the fact that they are arranged into chains of mutual services, a give and take extending over long periods of time and covering wide aspects of interest and activity. To this there is added the conspicuous and ceremonial manner in which most of the legal obligations have to be discharged. This binds people by an appeal to their vanity and self-regard, to their love of self-enhancement by display. Thus the binding force of these rules is due to the natural mental trend of self-interest, ambition and vanity, set into play by a special social mechanism into which the obligatory actions are framed.

With a wider and more elastic ' minimum definition ' of law, there is no doubt that new legal phenomena of the same type as those found in N.W. Melanesia will be discovered. There is no doubt that custom is not based only on a universal, undifferentiated, ubiquitous force, this mental inertia, though this unquestionably exists, and adds its quota to other constraint. There must be in all societies a class of rules too practical to be backed up by religious sanctions, too burdensome

to be left to mere goodwill, too personally vital to
individuals to be enforced by any abstract agency.
This is the domain of legal rules, and I venture to
foretell that reciprocity, systematic incidence, publicity
and ambition will be found to be the main factors in the
binding machinery of primitive law.

PART II

PRIMITIVE CRIME AND ITS PUNISHMENT

I

THE LAW IN BREACH AND THE RESTORATION OF ORDER

IT lies in the nature of scientific interest, which is but refined curiosity, that it turns more readily to the extraordinary and sensational than to the normal and matter-of-course. At first, in a new line of research or in a young branch of study, it is the exception, the apparent breach of the natural law, which attracts attention and gradually leads to the discovery of new universal regularities. For—and here lies the paradox of scientific passion—systematic study takes up the miraculous only to transform it into the natural. Science in the long run builds up a Universe well-regulated, founded on generally valid laws, driven by definite all-pervading forces, ordered according to a few fundamental principles.

Not that wonder, the romance of the marvellous and mysterious, should be banished by science from reality. The philosophic mind is ever kept on its course by the desire for new worlds and new experiences, and metaphysics lures us on by the promise of a vision beyond the rim of the furthest horizon. But the character of curiosity, the appreciation of what really is marvellous has been changed in the meantime by the discipline of science. The contemplation of the great lines of the world, the mystery of immediate data and ultimate ends, the meaningless impetus of 'creative evolution' make reality sufficiently tragic, mysterious, and questionable to the naturalist or student of culture, if he chooses to reflect upon the sum total of his knowledge and contemplate its limits. But to the mature scientific mind there can be no more thrills from the unexpected accident, no isolated sensation of a new, unrelated landscape in the exploration of reality. Every new discovery is but a step further on the same road, every new principle merely extends or shifts our old horizon.

Anthropology, still a young science, is now on the way to free itself from the control of pre-scientific interest, though certain recent attempts at offering extremely simple and, at the same time, sensational solutions of all the riddles of Culture are still dominated by crude curiosity. In the study of primitive law we can perceive this sound tendency in the gradual but definite recognition that savagery is not ruled by moods, passions, and accidents, but by tradition and order. Even then there remains something of the old 'shocker' interest in the over-emphasis of criminal justice, in the attention devoted to the breaches of the law and their punishment. Law in modern Anthropology is still almost exclusively studied in its singular and sensational manipulations, in cases of blood-curdling crime, followed by tribal vendetta, in accounts of criminal sorcery with retaliation, of incest, adultery, breach of taboo or murder. In all this, besides the dramatic piquancy of the incidents, the anthropologist can, or thinks he can, trace certain unexpected, exotic, astonishing features of primitive law : a transcending solidarity of the kindred group, excluding all sense of self-interest ; a legal and economic Communism ; a submission to a rigid, undifferentiated tribal law.[1]

As a reaction against the method and the principles just stated, I have tried to approach the facts of primitive law in the Trobriands from the other end. I have started with the description of the ordinary, not the singular ; of the law obeyed and not the law broken ; of the permanent currents and tides in their social life and not its adventitious storms. From the account given, I have been able to conclude that contrary to most established views civil law—or its savage

[1] Thus Rivers speaks of a " group sentiment of the clan system with its accompanying communistic practices ", supposed to exist in Melanesia, and he adds that to such natives the " principle ' each man for himself ' is beyond the reach of understanding " (*Social Organization*, p. 170). Sidney Hartland imagines that in savagery " The same code in the same Divine Name, and with equal authority, may make regulations for the conduct of commercial transactions and of the most intimate conjugal relations, as well as for a complex and splendid ceremonial of divine worship " (*Primitive Law*, p. 214). Both statements are misleading. Comp. also the quotations in Part I, Sections I and X.

equivalent—is extremely well developed, and that it rules all aspects of social organization. We also found that it is clearly distinguishable, and distinguished by the natives, from the other types of norm, whether morals or manners, rules of art or commands of religion. The rules of their law, far from being rigid, absolute or issued in the Divine Name, are maintained by social forces, understood as rational and necessary, elastic and capable of adjustment. Far also from being exclusively a group affair, his rights and his duties are in the main the concern of the individual, who knows perfectly well how to look after his interests and realizes that he has to redeem his obligations. We found indeed that the native's attitude towards duty and privilege is very much the same as in a civilized community—to the extent in fact that he not only stretches but also at times breaks the law. And this subject, not yet discussed, will claim our attention in these chapters. It would be a very one-sided picture indeed of the law in the Trobriands, if the rules were shown only in good working order, if the system were only described in equilibrium ! That law functions only very imperfectly, that there are many hitches and break-downs, I have now and again indicated, but a full description of the criminal and dramatic issues is necessary, though, as I have said, it should not be unduly emphasized.

There is still one reason why we must have a close look at native life in disorder. We found that in the Trobriands, social relations are governed by a number of legal principles. The most important of these is Mother-right, which rules that a child is bodily related and morally beholden by kinship to its mother and to her only. This principle governs succession to rank, power and dignities, economic inheritance, the rights to soil and to local citizenship and membership in the totemic clan. The status between brother and sister, the relations between the sexes and most of their private and public social intercourse is defined by rules forming part of matriarchal law. The economic duties of a man towards his married sister and her household constitute a strange and important feature of this law. The whole system is based on mythology, on the native theory of procreation, on certain of their magico-religious beliefs and it pervades all the institutions and customs of the tribe.

But, side by side with the system of Mother-right, in its shadow so to speak, there exist certain other, minor systems of legal rules. The law of marriage, defining the status of husband and wife, with its patrilocal arrangements, with its limited but clear bestowal of authority on the man and of guardianship over his wife and children in certain specified matters, is based on legal principles independent of Mother-right, though on several points intertwined with it and adjusted to it. The constitution of a village community, the position of the headman in his village and of the chief in his district, the privileges and duties of the public magician—all these are independent legal systems.

Now since we know that primitive law is not perfect, the problem emerges: how does this composite body of systems behave under the strain of circumstances ? Is each system well harmonized within its own limits ? Does such a system, moreover, keep within its limits or has it a tendency to encroach upon alien ground ? Do the systems then come into conflict, and what is the character of such conflict ? Here once more we have to appeal to the criminal, disorderly, disloyal elements of the community to furnish us with material from which we can answer our questions.

In the accounts to which we now proceed—and which will be given concretely and with some detail— we shall keep before us the main problems still unsolved : the nature of criminal acts and procedure and their relation to civil law ; the main factors active in the restitution of the disturbed equilibrium ; the relations and the possible conflicts between the several systems of native law.

While engaged in my field-work in the Trobriands, I used always to live right among the natives, pitching

PLATE V.

A conical heap of Yams is put up in front of a Chief's storehouse by his wife's relatives.
(*See* page **36**)

[*face* page **76.**]

my tent in the village, and being thus forcibly present at all that happened, trivial or solemn, hum-drum or dramatic. The event which I now proceed to relate happened during my first visit in the Trobriands, a few months only after I had started my field-work in the archipelago.

One day an outbreak of wailing and a great commotion told me that a death had occurred somewhere in the neighbourhood. I was informed that Kima'i, a young lad of my acquaintance, of sixteen or so, had fallen from a coco-nut palm and killed himself.

I hastened to the next village where this had occurred, only to find the whole mortuary proceedings in progress. This was my first case of death, mourning, and burial, so that in my concern with the ethnographical aspects of the ceremonial, I forgot the circumstances of the tragedy even though one or two singular facts occurred at the same time in the village which should have aroused my suspicions. I found that another youth had been severely wounded by some mysterious coincidence. And at the funeral there was obviously a general feeling of hostility between the village where the boy died and that into which his body was carried for burial.

Only much later was I able to discover the real meaning of these events : the boy had committed suicide. The truth was that he had broken the rules of exogamy, the partner in his crime being his maternal

cousin, the daughter of his mother's sister. This had
been known and generally disapproved of, but nothing
was done until the girl's discarded lover, who had
wanted to marry her and who felt personally injured,
took the initiative. This rival threatened first to use
black magic against the guilty youth, but this had not
much effect. Then one evening he insulted the
culprit in public—accusing him in the hearing of the
whole community of incest and hurling at him certain
expressions intolerable to a native.

For this there was only one remedy ; only one
means of escape remained to the unfortunate youth.
Next morning he put on festive attire and ornamentation, climbed a coco-nut palm and addressed the
community, speaking from among the palm leaves
and bidding them farewell. He explained the reasons
for his desperate deed and also launched forth a veiled
accusation against the man who had driven him to his
death, upon which it became the duty of his clansmen
to avenge him. Then he wailed aloud, as is the
custom, jumped from a palm some sixty feet high
and was killed on the spot. There followed a fight
within the village in which the rival was wounded ;
and the quarrel was repeated during the funeral.

Now this case opened up a number of important
lines of inquiry. I was here in the presence of a
pronounced crime : the breach of totemic clan
exogamy. The exogamous prohibition is one of the

corner-stones of totemism, mother-right, and the classificatory system of kinship. All females of his clan are called sisters by a man and forbidden as such. It is an axiom of Anthropology that nothing arouses a greater horror than the breach of this prohibition, and that besides a strong reaction of public opinion, there are also supernatural punishments, which visit this crime. Nor is this axiom devoid of foundation in fact. If you were to inquire into the matter among the Trobrianders, you would find that all statements confirm the axiom, that the natives show horror at the idea of violating the rules of exogamy and that they believe that sores, disease and even death might follow clan incest. This is the ideal of native law, and in moral matters it is easy and pleasant strictly to adhere to the ideal—when judging the conduct of others or expressing an opinion about conduct in general.

When it comes to the application of morality and ideals to real life, however, things take on a different complexion. In the case described it was obvious that the facts would not tally with the ideal of conduct. Public opinion was neither outraged by the knowledge of the crime to any extent, nor did it react directly—it had to be mobilized by a public statement of the crime and by insults being hurled at the culprit by an interested party. Even then he had to carry out the punishment himself. The

' group-reaction ' and the ' supernatural sanction '
were not therefore the active principles. Probing
further into the matter and collecting concrete
information, I found that the breach of exogamy—
as regards intercourse and not marriage—is by no
means a rare occurrence, and public opinion is lenient,
though decidedly hypocritical. If the affair is carried
on *sub rosa* with a certain amount of decorum, and if
no one in particular stirs up trouble—' public opinion '
will gossip, but not demand any harsh punishment.
If, on the contrary, scandal breaks out—every one
turns against the guilty pair and by ostracism and
insults one or the other may be driven to suicide.

As regards the supernatural sanction, this case led
me to an interesting and important discovery. I
learned that there is a perfectly well established
remedy against any pathological consequences of this
trespass, a remedy considered practically infallible,
if properly executed. That is to say the natives possess
a system of magic consisting of spells and rites
performed over water, herbs, and stones, which when
correctly carried out, is completely efficient in undoing
the bad results of clan incest.

That was the first time in my field-work that I came
across what could be called a well-established system
of evasion and that in the case of one of the most
fundamental laws of the tribe. Later on I discovered
that such parasitic growths upon the main branches

of tribal order exist in several other cases, besides the counteraction of incest. The importance of this fact is obvious. It shows clearly that a supernatural sanction need not safeguard a rule of conduct with an automatic effect. Against magical influence there may be counter-magic. It is no doubt better not to run the risk—the counter-magic may have been imperfectly learned or faultily performed—but the risk is not great. The supernatural sanction shows then a considerable elasticity, in conjunction with a suitable antidote.

This methodical antidote teaches us another lesson. In a community where laws are not only occasionally broken, but systematically circumvented by well-established methods, there can be no question of a 'spontaneous' obedience to law, of slavish adherence to tradition. For this tradition teaches man surreptitiously how to evade some of its sterner commands—and you cannot be *spontaneously* pushed forwards and pulled back at the same time !

Magic to undo the consequences of clan incest is perhaps the most definite instance of methodical evasion of law, but there are other cases besides. Thus a system of magic to estrange the affections of a woman from her husband and to induce her to commit adultery is a traditional way of flouting the institution of marriage and the prohibition of adultery. To a slightly different category perhaps belong the various forms of deleterious and malicious magic : to destroy the crops, to thwart a fisherman, to drive the pigs into the jungle, to blight bananas, coco-nuts or areca palms, to spoil a feast or a *Kula* expedition.   Such magic, being levelled at established institutions and important pursuits, is really an instrument of crime, supplied by tradition.   As such it is a department of tradition, which works against law and is directly in conflict with it, since law in various forms safeguards these pursuits and institutions.   The case of sorcery, which is a special and very important form of black magic, will be discussed presently, as also certain non-magical systems of evasion of tribal law.

The law of exogamy, the prohibition of marriage and intercourse within the clan is often quoted as one of the most rigid and wholesale commandments of primitive law, in that it forbids sexual relations within the clan with the same stringency, regardless of the degree of kinship between the two people concerned.   The unity of the clan and the reality of the ' classificatory system of relationship ' are—it is urged —most fully vindicated in the taboo of clan incest. It lumps together all the men and all the women of the clan as ' brothers ' and ' sisters ' to each other and debars them absolutely from sexual intimacy. A careful analysis of the relevant facts in the Trobriands completely disposes of this view.   It is again one of these figments of native tradition, taken over at its face value by anthropology and bodily incorporated into its teachings.[1] In the Trobriands, the breach of exogamy is regarded quite differently according to whether the guilty pair are closely related or whether they are only united by bonds of common clanship. Incest with a sister is to the natives an unspeakable, almost unthinkable crime—which again does not mean that it is never committed. The breach in the case of a matrilineal first cousin is a very serious offence, and it can have, as we have seen, tragic consequences. As kinship recedes, the stringency lessens and, when committed with one who merely belongs to the same clan, the breach of exogamy is but a venial offence, easily condoned. Thus, as regards this prohibition, the females of his clan are to a man not one compact group, not one homogeneous ' clan ', but a well-differentiated set of individuals, each standing in a special relation, according to her place in his genealogy.

[1] To give an illustration, reversing the rôle of savage and civilized, of ethnographer and informant : many of my Melanesian friends, taking at its face value the doctrine of ' brotherly love ' preached by Christian Missionaries and the taboo on warfare and killing preached and promulgated by Government officials, were unable to reconcile the stories about the Great War, reaching—through planters, traders, overseers, plantation hands—the remotest Melanesian or Papuan village. They were really puzzled at hearing that in one day white men were wiping out as many of their own kind as would make up several of the biggest Melanesian tribes. They forcibly concluded that the White Man was a tremendous liar, but they were not certain at which end the lie lay—whether in the moral pretence or in his bragging about war achievements.

From the point of view of the native libertine, *suvasova* (the breach of exogamy) is indeed a specially interesting and spicy form of erotic experience. Most of my informants would not only admit but actually did boast about having committed this offence or that of adultery (*kaylasi*) ; and I have many concrete, well-attested cases on record.

So far I have spoken of intercourse. Marriage within the same clan is a much more serious affair. Nowadays even, with the general relaxation of the rigour of traditional law, there are only some two or three cases of marriage within the clan in existence, the most notorious being that of Modulabu, headman of the large village of Obweria, with Ipwaygana, a renowned witch, who is also suspected of intercourse with the *tauva'u*, supernatural evil spirits who bring disease. Both of these people belong to the Malasi clan. It is remarkable that this clan is traditionally associated with incest. There is a myth of brother and sister incest, which is the source of love magic, and this happened in the Malasi clan. The most notorious case of brother-sister incest of recent times also occurred in this clan.[1] Thus the relation of actual life to the ideal state of affairs, as mirrored in traditional morals and law, is very instructive.

[1] For an ampler account of this subject, see the writer's article on " Complex and Myth in Mother-right ", *Psyche*, vol. v, No. 3, Jan., 1925 ; reprinted in op. cit., *Sex and Repression in Savage Society*, uniform with this work.

II

SORCERY AND SUICIDE AS LEGAL INFLUENCES

IN the preceding section I have described a case of breach of tribal law and discussed the nature of criminal tendencies as well as of the forces which set about to restore order and tribal equilibrium as soon as it has been upset.

We touched in our account upon two incidents—the use of sorcery as means of coercion and the practice of suicide as expiation and challenge. A more detailed discussion must now be devoted to these two subjects. Sorcery is practised in the Trobriands by a limited number of specialists—as a rule men of outstanding intelligence and personality, who acquire the art by learning a number of spells and submitting to certain conditions. They exercise their power on their own behalf, and also professionally for a fee. Since the belief in sorcery is deeply rooted and every serious sickness and death is attributed to black magic, the sorcerer is held in great awe, and, at first sight, his position lends itself inevitably to abuse and blackmail. It has been in fact frequently affirmed that sorcery is the main criminal agency, as regards Melanesia and

G

elsewhere.   Speaking of the region I know from
personal experience, N.W. Melanesia, this view represents one side of the picture.   Sorcery gives a man
power, wealth, and influence ;   and this he uses to
further his own ends, but the very fact that he has
much to lose and little to gain by flagrant abuses makes
him as a rule very moderate.   The chief, the notables,
and the other sorcerers watch over him carefully ;
moreover not infrequently one sorcerer is believed to
be put away by another on behalf of a chief and by the
chief's orders.

As regards his services, sold professionally, those in
power—chiefs, men of rank and wealth—have again
the first claim on him.   When appealed to by lesser
people, the sorcerer would not lend himself to unjust
or fantastic requests.   He is too rich and big a man to
do anything outside the law and he can afford to be
honest and just.   When a real injustice or a thoroughly
unlawful act is to be punished on the other hand, the
sorcerer feels the weight of public opinion with him
and he is ready to champion a good cause and to receive
his full fee.   In such cases also the victim, on learning
that a sorcerer is at work against him, may quail
and make amends or come to an equitable arrangement.
Thus ordinarily, black magic acts as a genuine legal
force, for it is used in carrying out the rules of tribal
law, it prevents the use of violence and restores
equilibrium.

An interesting denouement, illustrating the legal
aspect of sorcery, is furnished by the custom of finding
out the reasons for which a man has been killed by
witchcraft. This is achieved by the correct interpreta-
tion of certain marks or symptoms to be seen on the
exhumed body. Some 12 to 24 hours after the pre-
liminary burial, at the first subsequent sunset, the
grave is opened, the body washed, anointed and
examined. The custom has been forbidden by Government Orders—it is ' disgusting ' to the white man,
who anyhow has no opportunity nor any business to
be there—but it is still surreptitiously practised in
remoter villages. I have assisted several times at an
exhumation and once, when it was done somewhat
earlier, before the sun had set, I was able to obtain
photographs. The proceedings are highly dramatic.
A throng presses round the grave, some people rapidly
remove the earth amid loud wailing, others intone
magical spells against *mulukwausi* (corpse-devouring
and man-killing flying witches) and spit over all those
present with chewed ginger. As they come nearer the
bundle of mats enshrouding the corpse, they wail and
chant louder and louder, until the body is uncovered
amid an outburst of screams and the throng sweep
and press nearer. All urge forward to see it, wooden
platters with coco-nut cream are given to those nearest
to wash the body with, ornaments are taken off the
corpse, it is rapidly washed, wrapped up again and

buried. During the time it is out the marks have to
be registered. It is not a formal affair and differences
of opinion are frequent. Often there are no clear
marks and still more often people cannot agree in their
verdict.

But there are marks (*kala wabu*) about which there
can be no doubt, which unequivocally indicate a habit,
propensity or characteristic of the dead one, which had
provoked the hostility of some one who had then
commissioned a sorcerer to kill the victim. If the body
shows scratches, especially on the shoulder, similar to
kimali, the erotic scratches impressed during sexual
dalliance, this means that deceased has been guilty
of adultery or has been too successful with women, to
the annoyance of a chief, man of power, or a sorcerer.
This frequent cause of death produces also other
symptoms : the exhumed body is found with the
legs apart ; or with the mouth pursed, as if to emit
the smacking sound used to call a desired person
to a secret tryst. Or again the body is found swarming
with lice, since lousing one another is a favourite tender
occupation of lovers. Sometimes certain symptoms
appear before death : the other day a dying man was
observed to move his arm to and fro in a beckoning
gesture, and lo ! after his body was exhumed there
were *kimali* marks on the shoulders. Again in another
concrete case, the dying man was heard to emit a
smacking sound, and later on at exhumation he

swarmed with lice. It had been notorious that this man had allowed himself to be loused in public by some of the wives of Numakala, one of the former paramount chiefs of Kiriwina—and he had been obviously punished by high order.

When signs are discovered which suggest decoration, face painting or certain dancing ornamentations, or when the corpse's hand trembles, as does the master-dancer's in wielding the *kaydebu* (dancing shield) or the *bisila* (bunch of pandanus leaves)—his personal beauty or those achievements which gain favour with the fair sex had set sorcery against the defunct Don Juan. Red, black and white hues on the skin, patterns suggestive of the designs on a noble's house and store, swellings like the beams of a rich yam-house— signify that the dead one indulged in too ambitious decorations of his hut or store, and thus aroused the chief's resentment. Taro-shaped tumours or an inordinate craving for this vegetable shortly before death indicate that deceased had too splendid taro-gardens or did not pay sufficient tribute of this commodity to the chief. Bananas, coco-nuts, sugar-cane produce *mutatis mutandis* similar effects, while betel-nut colours the mouth of the corpse red. If the body is found foaming at the mouth, it shows that the man was too much addicted to opulent and ostentatious eating or bragging about food. A loose skin, peeling off in folds means in particular abuse of pork diet or dishonest dealing in the stewardship of pigs, which are the chief's monopoly and only given into the care of lesser men. The chief also resents it when a man has not kept to the ceremonial and not bent before him low enough ; such a man will be found doubled up in his grave. Putrid matter flowing in strings out of the nostrils represents, in this post-mortem sorcery code, the valuable necklaces of shell-discs and thus too great a success in the *Kula* trade ; while circular swellings on the arms indicate the same through the means of *mwali* (armshells). Finally, a man killed for the reason that he is a sorcerer himself, produces, besides the normal spirit (*baloma*), also a material ghost (*kousi*), which spooks round the grave and plays various pranks.[1] The body of a sorcerer is also often found disarranged, distorted in the grave.

I have obtained this list by discussing concrete cases and noting symptoms actually registered. It is very important to realize that frequently, I should say in most cases, no signs are found on the body or there is no agreement about them. Needless to say, a sick man always suspects, in fact thinks he knows who is the sorcerer guilty of his ailment, on whose behalf he acts and for what reason. So that the ' finding '

---

[1] Compare the article on ' Baloma ' in the *Journal of the Royal Anthrop. Inst.*, 1916, where I describe the beliefs in the two surviving principles in detail, without mentioning that the *kousi* is found exclusively in the case of a sorcerer. This I found out during my third expedition to New Guinea.

of a mark has all the characters of an *a posteriori* verification of what is already known. In this light, the above list, which includes the ' causes of death ' openly discussed and readily found, receives a special significance : it shows us which offences are not altogether considered dishonourable or contemptible, and also those which are not too burdensome on the survivors. In fact sexual success, beauty, skill in dancing, ambition for wealth and recklessness in display and in the enjoyment of worldly goods, too much power by sorcery—these are enviable failings or sins, dangerous, since they arouse the jealousy of the mighty, but surrounding the culprit with a halo of glory. On the other hand, since almost all these offences are resented by the chief of the district, rightly resented at that and legally punished, the survivors are relieved of the burdensome duty of vendetta.

The point of real importance in our argument, however, is that all these standard symptoms show us how much resented is any prominence, any excess of qualities or possessions not warranted by social position, any outstanding personal achievement or virtue not associated with rank or power. These things are punishable and the one who watches over the mediocrity of others is the chief, whose essential privilege and duty to tradition is to enforce the golden mean upon others. The chief, however, cannot use direct bodily violence in such matters, when only a suspicion

or a shade of doubt or a tendency tell against the
delinquent. The proper legal means for him is to resort
to sorcery and be it remembered he has to pay for it
out of his private purse. He was allowed to use violence
(i.e. before white man's ' orders ' came in), to punish
any direct breach of etiquette or ceremonial as well as
flagrant offences, such as adultery with any of his wives,
theft of his private possessions or any personal insult.
A man who would dare to place himself above the chief's
head, to touch that tabooed part of his neck or
shoulders, to use certain filthy expressions in his presence,
to commit such breach of etiquette as sexually to allude
to his sister—would have been immediately speared by
one of the chief's armed attendants. This applies in
full stringency to the paramount chief of Kiriwina
only. Cases are on record in which by an accident a
man offended the chief, and had to fly for his life. A
recent case is that of a man who during warfare from
the opposite camp had hurled an insult at the chief.
This man was actually killed after peace had been
concluded, and his death was regarded as a just
retribution for his offence and no vendetta followed.

We can see thus that in many, in fact in most
cases, black magic is regarded as the chief's principal
instrument in the enforcement of his exclusive
privileges and prerogatives. Such cases pass, of course,
imperceptibly into actual oppression and crass injustice,
of which I could mention also a number of concrete

instances. Even then, since it invariably ranges itself on the side of the powerful, wealthy, and influential, sorcery remains a support of vested interest ; hence in the long run, of law and order. It is always a conservative force, and it furnishes really the main source of the wholesome fear of punishment and retribution indispensable in any orderly society. There is hardly anything more pernicious, therefore, in the many European ways of interference with savage peoples, than the bitter animosity with which Missionary, Planter, and Official alike pursue the sorcerer.[1] The rash, haphazard, unscientific application of our morals, laws, and customs to native societies, and the destruction of native law, quasi-legal machinery and instruments of power leads only to anarchy and moral atrophy and in the long run to the extinction of culture and race.

Sorcery, in fine, is neither exclusively a method of administering justice, nor a form of criminal practice. It can be used both ways, though it is never employed in direct opposition to law, however often it might be used to commit wrongs against a weaker man on behalf of a more powerful. In whatever way it works, it is a way of emphasizing the *status quo*, a method of

[1] The sorcerer, who stands for conservatism, the old tribal order, the old beliefs and apportionment of power, naturally resents the innovators and the destroyers of his *Weltanschauung*. He is as a rule the natural enemy of the white man, who therefore hates him.

expressing the traditional inequalities and of counter-
acting the formation of any new ones.   Since conservatism is the most important trend in a primitive
society, sorcery on the whole is a beneficent agency, of
enormous value for early culture.

These considerations show clearly how difficult it
is to draw a line between the quasi-legal and quasi-
criminal applications of sorcery.   The ' criminal '
aspect of law in savage communities is perhaps even
vaguer than the ' civil ' one, the idea of ' justice ' in
our sense hardly applicable and the means of restoring
a disturbed tribal equilibrium slow and cumbersome.

Having   learnt   something   about   Trobriand
criminology from the study of sorcery, let us now pass
to suicide.   Though by no means a purely juridical
institution, suicide possesses incidentally a distinct
legal aspect.   It is practised by two serious methods
lo'u (jumping off a palm top) and the taking of
irremediable poison from the gall bladder of a globe-
fish (*soka*) ; and by the milder method of partaking
of some of the vegetable poison *tuva*, used for stunning
fish.   A generous dose of emetic restores to life one
poisoned by *tuva*, which is therefore used in lovers'
quarrels, matrimonial differences, and similar cases,
of which several occurred during my stay in the
Trobriands, none fatal.

The two fatal forms of suicide are used as means of
escape from situations without an issue and the

underlying mental attitude is somewhat complex, embracing the desire of self-punishment, revenge, re-habilitation, and sentimental grievance. A number of concrete cases briefly described will illustrate best the psychology of suicide.

A case somewhat similar to that of Kima'i, described above, was that of a girl, Bomawaku, who was in love with a youth of her own clan and had an official and acceptable suitor, for whom she did not care. She lived in her *bukumatula* (unmarried peoples' dormitory), built for her by her father and received there her unlawful lover. Her suitor discovered this, insulted her in public, upon which she put on festive dress and ornamentation, wailed from the palm top, and jumped off. This is an old story, told me by an eye-witness, in reminiscence of the Kima'i event. The girl had also sought an escape from an intolerable impasse, into which her passion and the traditional prohibitions had placed her. But the immediate and the real cause of the suicide was the moment of insult. If not for that, the deeper but less poignant conflict between love and taboo would never have led to a rash act.

Mwakenuwa of Liluta, a man of high rank, great magical powers, and outstanding personality, whose fame has reached down to our times across a couple of generations, had among other wives one Isowa'i, to whom he was very attached. He used to quarrel with her sometimes and one day in the course of a violent dissention he insulted her by one of the worst formulæ (*kwoy lumuta*) which, especially from husband to wife, is regarded as unbearable.[1] Isowa'i acted up to the traditional idea of honour and committed suicide on the spot by *lo'u* (jumping off a palm). Next day, while the wailing for Isowa'i was in progress, Mwakenuwa followed her and his corpse was placed beside hers to be bewailed together. Here it was rather a matter of passion than of law. But the case well shows how strongly the traditional feeling and sense of honour was averse to any excess, to any transgression of the even calm tone. It shows also how strongly the survivor could be moved by the self-inflicted fate of the one who had taken her life.

A similar case occurred some time ago, in which the husband accused his wife of adultery, upon which she jumped off a palm and he followed her. Another event of more recent date, was the suicide by poisoning of Isakapu of Sinaketa, accused by her husband of adultery. Bogonela, a wife of the chief Kouta'uya of Sinaketa, discovered guilty of misconduct during his absence by a fellow wife, committed suicide on the spot. A few years ago in Sinaketa a man pestered by one of his wives, who accused him of adultery and other transgressions, committed suicide by poisoning.

[1] For an account and analysis of abuse and obscene expressions, cf. op. cit., *Sex and Repression in Savage Society* or the writer's article in *Psyche*, v. 3, 1925.

Bolubese, wife of one of the previous paramount chiefs of Kiriwina, ran away from her husband to her own village, and threatened by her own kinsmen (maternal uncle and brothers) to be sent back by force, killed herself by *lo'u*. There came to my notice a number of similar cases, illustrating the tensions between husband and wife, between lovers, between kinsmen.

Two motives must be registered in the psychology of suicide : first, there is always some sin, crime or passionate outburst to expiate, whether a breach of exogamous rules, or adultery, or an unjust injury done, or an attempt to escape one's obligations ; secondly, there is a protest against those who have brought this trespass to light, insulted the culprit in public, forced him into an unbearable situation. One of these two motives may be at times more prominent than the other, but as a rule there is a mixture of both in equal proportions. The person publicly accused admits his or her guilt, takes all the consequences, carries out the punishment upon his own person, but at the same time declares that he has been badly treated, appeals to the sentiment of those who have driven him to the extreme if they are his friends or relations, or if they are his enemies appeals to the solidarity of his kinsmen, asking them to carry on a vendetta (*lugwa*).

Suicide is certainly not a means of administering

justice, but it affords the accused and oppressed one—
whether he be guilty or innocent—a means of escape
and rehabilitation. It looms large in the psychology
of the natives, is a permanent damper on any violence
of language or behaviour, on any deviation from custom
or tradition, which might hurt or offend another.
Thus suicide, like sorcery, is a means of keeping the
natives to the strict observance of the law, a means of
preventing people from extreme and unusual types
of behaviour.   Both are pronounced conservative
influences and as such are strong supports of law and
order.

What have we learned from the facts of crime
and its punishment recorded in this and the foregoing chapters? We have found that the principles
according to which crime is punished are very vague,
that the methods of carrying out retribution are fitful,
governed by chance and personal passion rather than
by any system of fixed institutions.   The most
important methods, in fact, are a bye-product of non-
legal institutions, customs, arrangements and events
such as sorcery and suicide, the power of the chief,
magic, the supernatural consequences of taboo and
personal acts of vindictiveness. These institutions and
usages, far from being legal in their main function, only
very partially and imperfectly subserve the end of
maintaining and enforcing the biddings of tradition.
We have not found any arrangement or usage which

could be classed as a form of ' administration of justice ', according to a code and by fixed methods. All the legally effective institutions we found are rather means of cutting short an illegal or intolerable state of affairs, of restoring the equilibrium in social life and of giving vent to the feelings of oppression and injustice felt by individuals. Crime in the Trobriand society can be but vaguely defined—it is sometimes an outburst of passion, sometimes the breach of a definite taboo, sometimes an attempt on person or property (murder, theft, assault), sometimes an indulgence in too high ambitions or wealth, not sanctioned by tradition, in conflict with the prerogatives of the chief or some notable. We have also found that the most definite prohibitions are elastic, since there exist methodical systems of evasion.

I shall now proceed to the discussion of instances in which law is not broken by an act of definitely illegal nature, but where it is confronted by a system of legalized usage, almost as strong as traditional law itself.

III

SYSTEMS OF LAW IN CONFLICT

PRIMITIVE law is not a homogeneous, perfectly unified body of rules, based upon one principle developed into a consistent system. So much we know already from our previous survey of legal facts in the Trobriand Islands. The law of these natives consists on the contrary of a number of more or less independent systems, only partially adjusted to one another. Each of these—matriarchy, father-right, the law of marriage, the prerogatives and duties of a chief and so on—has a certain field completely its own, but it can also trespass beyond its legitimate boundaries. This results in a state of tense equilibrium with an occasional outbreak. The study of the mechanism of such conflicts between legal principles, whether overt or masked, is extremely instructive and it reveals to us the very nature of the social fabric in a primitive tribe. I shall therefore proceed now to the description of one or two occurrences and then to their analysis.

I shall describe first a dramatic event which illustrates the conflict between the main principle of law, Mother-right, and one of the strongest sentiments, paternal love, round which there cluster many usages, tolerated by custom, though in reality working against the law.

The two principles Mother-right and Father-love are focussed most sharply in the relation of a man to his sister's son and to his own son respectively. His matrilineal nephew is his nearest kinsman and the legal heir to all his dignities and offices. His own son on the other hand is not regarded as a kinsman; legally he is not related to his father, and the only bond is the sociological status of marriage with the mother.[1]

Yet in the reality of actual life the father is much more attached to his own son than to his nephew. Between father and son there obtains invariably friendship and personal attachment; between uncle and nephew not infrequently the ideal of perfect solidarity is marred by the rivalries and suspicions inherent in any relationship of succession.

Thus the powerful legal system of Mother-right is associated with a rather weak sentiment, while Father-love, much less important in law, is backed by a strong personal feeling. In the case of a chief whose power is considerable, the personal influence outweighs the ruling of the law and the position of the son is as strong as that of the nephew.

That was the case in the capital village of Omarakana, the residence of the principal chief, whose

---

[1] Cf. *The Father in Primitive Psychology* (1926), originally published in *Psyche*, vol. iv, No. 2.

H

power extends over the whole district, whose influence reaches many archipelagoes, and whose fame is spread all over the eastern end of New Guinea. I soon found out that there was a standing feud between his sons and nephews, a feud which assumed a really acute form in the ever recurrent quarrels between his favourite son Namwana Guya'u and his second eldest nephew Mitakata.

The final outbreak came when the chief's son inflicted a serious injury on the nephew in a litigation before the resident government official of the district. Mitakata, the nephew, was in fact convicted and put to prison for a month or so.

When the news of this reached the village, the short exultation among the partisans of Namwana Guya'u was followed by a panic, for everyone felt that things had come to a crisis. The chief shut himself up in his personal hut, full of evil forebodings of the consequences for his favourite, who was felt to have acted rashly and in outrage of tribal law and feeling. The kinsmen of the imprisoned young heir to chieftainship were boiling with suppressed anger and indignation. As night fell, the subdued village settled down to a silent supper, each family over its solitary meal. There was nobody on the central place—Namwana Guya'u was not to be seen, the chief To'uluwa hid in his hut, most of his wives and their families also remained indoors. Suddenly a loud voice rang out across the silent village.

Bagido'u, the heir apparent, and eldest brother of the imprisoned man, standing before his hut, spoke out, addressing the offender of his family :—

" Namwana Guya'u, you are a cause of trouble. We, the Tabalu of Omarakana, allowed you to stay here, to live among us. You had plenty of food in Omarakana, you ate of our food, you partook of the pigs brought to us as a tribute and of the fish. You sailed in our canoe. You built a hut on our soil. Now you have done us harm. You have told lies. Mitakata is in prison. We do not want you to stay here. This is our village! You are a stranger here. Go away! We chase you away! We chase you out of Omarakana."

These words were uttered in a loud piercing voice, trembling with strong emotion, each short sentence spoken after a pause, each like an individual missile, hurled across the empty space to the hut where Namwana Guya'u sat brooding. After that the younger sister of Mitakata also arose and spoke, and then a young man, one of the maternal nephews. Their words were almost the same as in the first speech, the burden being the formula of chasing away, the *yoba*. The speeches were received in deep silence. Nothing stirred in the village. But, before the night was over, Namwana Guya'u had left Omarakana for ever. He had gone over and settled in his own village, in Osapola the village whence his mother came, a few miles distant. For weeks his mother and sister wailed for him with the loud lamentations of mourning for the dead. The chief remained for three days in his hut, and when he came out looked older and broken up by grief. All his personal interest and affection were on the side of his favourite son, of course. Yet he could do nothing to help him. His kinsmen had acted in complete accordance with their rights and, according to tribal law, he could not possibly dissociate himself from them. No power could change the decree of exile. Once the ' Go away '—(*bukula*), ' we chase thee away '—(*kayabaim*), were pronounced, the man had to go. These words, very rarely uttered in dead earnest, have a binding force and almost ritual power when pronounced by the citizens of a place against a resident outsider. A man who would try to brave the dreadful insult involved in them and remain in spite of them, would be dishonoured for ever. In fact, anything but immediate compliance with a ritual request is unthinkable for a Trobriand Islander.

The chief's resentment against his kinsmen was deep and lasting. At first he would not even speak to them. For a year or so, not one of them dared to ask to be taken on overseas expeditions by him, although they were fully entitled to this privilege. Two years later in 1917, when I returned to the Trobriands, Namwana Guya'u was still resident in the other village and keeping aloof from his father's kinsmen, though he frequently

PLATE VI.

A Ceremonial Act of the Kula before the Chief's personal hut at Omarakana.
The Ethnographer's tent in the background.   (*See* page 25.)

[*face* page 104.]

paid visits to Omarakana in order to be in attendance on his father, especially when To'uluwa went abroad. The mother had died within a year after the expulsion. As the natives described it : " She wailed and wailed, refused to eat, and died." The relations between the two main enemies were completely broken and Mitakata, the young chieftain who had been imprisoned, had sent away his wife who belonged to the same sub-clan as Namwana Guya'u. There was a deep rift in the whole social life of Kiriwina.

The incident was one of the most dramatic events which I have ever witnessed in the Trobriands. I have described it at length, as it contains a clear illustration of Mother-right, of the power of tribal law and of the passions which work in spite of it.

The case though exceptionally dramatic and telling is by no means anomalous. In every village where there is a chief of high rank, an influential notable or a powerful sorcerer, he favours his sons and allows them privileges, which are, strictly speaking, not theirs. Often this produces no antagonisms within the community— when both son and nephew are moderate and tactful. Kayla'i, the son of M'tabalu, the recently deceased chief of highest rank of Kasanai, lives on in his father's village, carries on most of the communal magic and is on excellent terms with his father's successor. In the cluster of villages of Sinaketa, where there reside several chiefs of high rank, some of the son-favourites are good friends with the rightful heirs, some in open hostility to them.

In Kavataria, the village adjoining the Mission and the Government Station, the last chief's son, one Dayboya, has completely ousted the real masters, supported in this by European influence, which naturally worked for patrilineal claims. But the conflict, more acute nowadays and carried on with greater force by the paternal principle, because of the backing it inevitably receives from the white man, is as old as mythological tradition. It is expressed in the stories told for amusement, the *kukwanebu*, where *latula guya'u*, the chief's son, is a standard type, arrogant, pampered, pretentious, often the butt of practical jokes. In serious myths, he is sometimes the villain, sometimes the contending hero—but the opposition of the two principles is clearly marked. But most convincing as to the age and cultural depth of the conflict, is the fact that it is embedded in a number of institutions, with which we shall presently become acquainted. Among the people of low rank, the opposition between Mother-right and Father-love also exists, and it shows itself in the father's tendency to do all he can for his son, at the nephew's expense. And again after the father's death the son has to return to the heirs practically all the benefits and possessions received during the father's lifetime. This naturally leads to a good deal of discontent, friction, and round-about methods of arriving at a satisfactory settlement.

We are, then, once more face to face with the discrepancy between the ideal of law and its realization, between the orthodox version and the practice of actual life. We have already met with it in exogamy, in the system of counter-magic, in the relation between sorcery and law, and, indeed, in the elasticity of all the rules of civil law. Here, however, we find the very foundations of the tribal constitution challenged, indeed systematically flouted by a tendency entirely incompatible with it. Mother-right as we know is the most important and the most comprehensive principle of law, underlying all their customs and institutions. It rules that kinship has to be counted through females only and that all social privileges follow the maternal line. Thus it excludes the legal validity of a direct bodily tie between father and child and of any filiation in virtue of this tie.[1] With all this, the father loves the

---

[1] The natives are ignorant of the fact of physiological fatherhood, and, as I have shown in op. cit., *The Father in Primitive Psychology*, 1926, have a supernatural theory of the causes of birth. There is no physical continuity between the male and the children of his wife. Yet the father loves his child even from birth—to the extent at least to which the normal European father does. Since this cannot be due to any ideas that they are his offspring, this must be due to the outcome of some innate tendency in the human species, on the part of the male to feel attached to the children born by a woman with whom he is mated, has been living permanently and has kept watch over during her pregnancy. This appears to me the only plausible explanation of the ' voice

child invariably and this sentiment finds a limited recognition in law ; the husband has the right and duty to act as a guardian to his wife's children till puberty. This, of course, is the only line which law can possibly take in a culture with patrilocal marriage. Since small children cannot be severed from the mother, since she has to be with her husband, often at a distance from her own people, since she and her children need a male guardian and protector on the spot—the husband necessarily fulfils this rôle and he does it by strict and orthodox law. The same law, however, orders the boy— not the girl, who remains with the parents till marriage—to leave the father's house at puberty and to move to his mother's community and pass into the tutelage of his maternal uncle. This, on the whole, runs counter to the wishes of the father, of the son and of the latter's uncle—the three men concerned, with the result that there has grown a number of usages, tending to prolong paternal authority and to establish an additional bond between father and son. The strict law declares that the son is citizen of the maternal village, that in his father's he is but a stranger (*tomakava*)—usage allows him to remain there and to enjoy most of the privileges of citizenship.   For

of blood ' which speaks in societies ignorant of fatherhood as well as those that are emphatically patriarchal, which makes a father love his physiologically own child as well as one born through adultery—as long as he does not know of it. The tendency is of the greatest use to the species.

ceremonial purposes, in a funeral or mourning performance, in a feast and as a rule in fight, he will stand side by side with his maternal uncle. In daily execution of nine-tenths of all the pursuits and interests of life he is bound to his father.

The usage of keeping the son after puberty, often after marriage, is a regular institution : there exist definite arrangements to meet it, it is done according to strict rules and definite procedure, which make the usage anything but clandestine and irregular. There is first the accredited pretext that the son remains there to be able better to fill his father's yam-house, which he does in the name of his mother's brother and as his successor. In the case of a chief again there are certain offices, considered to be most appropriately filled by the chief's own son. When this latter marries he builds a house on his father's site, near the father's own dwelling.

The son naturally has to live and eat, he must therefore make gardens and carry on other pursuits. The father gives him a few *baleko* (garden plots) from his own lands, gives him a place in his canoe, grants him rights of fishing—hunting is of no importance in the Trobriands—equips him with tools, nets and other fishing tackle. As a rule, the father goes further. He allows his son certain privileges and gives him presents, which by right he should keep till he hands them on to his heirs. It is true that he will give such privileges and

presents to his heirs during his life-time, when they
solicit it by a payment called *pokala*. He cannot even
refuse the deal.   But then his younger brother or his
nephew has substantially to pay for land, magic,
Kula rights, heirlooms, or ' mastership ' in dances and
ceremonies ; even though they belong to him by right
and he would inherit them in any case. Now established
usage allows the man to give such valuables or privileges
to the son *free of charge*.   So that here the usage,
established but non-legal, not only takes great liberties
with the law, but adds insult to injury by granting the
usurper considerable advantages over the rightful
owner.

The most important arrangement by which a
temporary father-line is smuggled into Mother-right
is the institution of cross-cousin marriage. A man in
the Trobriands who has a son and whose sister gives
birth to a girl child has the right to ask that this infant
be betrothed to his son. Thus his grandchildren will be
of his own kin, and his son will become the brother-in-
law of the heir to chieftainship. This latter will, therefore, be under an obligation to supply the son's household with food and in general to be a helpmate to his
brother-in-law and protector of his sister's family.
Thus the very man on whose interest the son is likely
to encroach is prevented from resenting it and, indeed,
made to regard it as his own privilege. Cross-cousin
marriage in the Trobriands is an institution by

which a man can secure for his son a definite though roundabout right to remain for life in the father's community,   through   an   exceptional   matrilocal marriage, and enjoy almost all the privileges of full citizenship.

Thus round the sentiment of Father-love there crystallizes a number of established usages, sanctioned by tradition and regarded as the most natural course by the community. Yet they are contrary to strict law or involve exceptional and anomalous proceeding such as matrilocal marriage. If opposed and protested against in the name of the law, they must give way to it. Cases are on record, when the son, even though married to his father's niece, had to leave the community. And not infrequently the heirs put a stop to their uncle's illegal generosity, by demanding with *pokala* what he is about to give to his son. But any such opposition gives offence to the man in power, provokes hostilities and frictions, and is resorted to only in extreme cases.

IV

THE FACTORS OF SOCIAL COHESION IN A PRIMITIVE TRIBE

IN analysing the clash between Mother-right and Father-love, we have focussed our attention on the personal relations between the man, his son and his nephew respectively. But the problem is also that of the unity of the clan. For the group of two formed by the man in power (whether chief, notable, village headman, or sorcerer) and his heir is the very core of the matrilineal clan. The unity, homogeneity, and solidarity of the clan can be no greater than that of its core, and since we find that this core is fissured, that there are normally tensions and antagonisms between the two men, we cannot accept the axiom that the clan is a perfectly welded unit. But the ' clan-dogma ' or ' sib-dogma ', to use Dr. Lowie's apposite expression, is not without its foundations, and though we have shown that in its very nucleus the clan is split, and also that it is not homogeneous as regards exogamy, it will be good to show exactly how much truth there is in the contention of clan unity.

It may be stated at once that here, again, Anthropology has taken over the orthodox native doctrine or rather their legal fiction at its face value, and has been thus duped by mistaking the legal ideal for the sociological realities of tribal life. The position of native law in this matter is consistent and clear. Accepting Mother-right as the exclusive principle of kinship in legal matters, and applying it to its furthest consequences, the native divides all human beings into those connected with himself by the matrilineal tie whom he calls kinsmen (*veyola*), and those who are not thus related, and whom he calls strangers (*tomakava*). This doctrine then is combined with the ' classificatory principle of Kinship ', which fully governs only the vocabulary, but to a limited extent also influences legal relations. Both Mother-right and the classificatory principle are further associated with the totemic system, by which all human beings fall into four clans, subdivided further into an irregular number of sub-clans. A man or woman is a Malasi, Lukuba, Lukwasisiga, or Lukulabuta, of such and such sub-clan, and this totemic identity is as fixed and definite as sex, colour of skin, or size of body ; it does not cease with death, the spirit remaining what the man has been, and it existed before birth, the ' spirit-child ' being already member of a clan and sub-clan. Member-ship in sub-clan means a common ancestress, unity of kinship, unity of citizenship in a local community, common title to lands and co-operation in many economic and in all ceremonial activities. Legally it implies the fact of common clan and sub-clan name, common responsibilities in vendetta (*lugwa*), the rule of exogamy, finally the fiction of an overweening interest in one another's welfare, so that by a death the sub-clan first and to some extent the clan are considered bereft and the whole mourning ritual is tuned to this traditional view. The unity of the clan and still more of the sub-clan is, however, expressed most tangibly in the great festive distributions (*sagali*), in which the totemic groups play a game of ceremonially-economic give and take. Thus there is a multiple and a real unity of interests, activities and necessarily some feelings, uniting the members of a sub-clan and the component sub-clans into a clan and this fact is very strongly emphasized in many institutions, in mythology, in vocabulary and in the current sayings and traditional maxims.

But there is also the other side to the picture, of which we have had clear indications already, and this we must concisely formulate. First of all, though all *ideas* about kinship, totemic division, unity of substance, social duties, etc., tend to emphasize the ' clan dogma ', not all the *sentiments* follow this lead. While in any contest of social, political, or ceremonial nature a man through ambition, pride, and patriotism invariably sides with his matrilineal kindred, softer feelings, loving friendship, attachments make him often neglect clan for wife, children, and friends, in the ordinary situations of life. Linguistically, the term *veyogu* (my kinsman) has an emotional colouring of cold duty and pride, the term *lubaygu* (my friend and my sweetheart), on the other hand, possesses a distinctly warmer, more intimate tone. In their after death beliefs, too, the ties of love, conjugal attachment and friendship are made—in a less orthodox but more personal belief—to endure into the spirit world, even as totemic identity endures.

As to the definite duties of the clan, we have seen in detail, on the example of exogamy, how much elasticity, evasion, and breach there is. In economic matters as we know already, the exclusiveness of clan co-operation suffers a serious leakage through the father's tendency to give to his son and to take him into clan enterprises. *Lugwa* (the vendetta) is carried out but seldom : the payment of *lula* (peace-making price) is again a traditional form of compensation for, really of evasion of the sterner duty. In sentiment, the father or the widow is often far more keen on avenging the murdered one's death than his kinsmen are. On all occasions when the clan acts as one economic unit in ceremonial distributions, it remains homogeneous only with regard to other clans. Within, strict accounts are kept between the component sub-clans and within the sub-clan between individuals. Thus here again the unity exists on one side, but it is combined on the other with a thorough-going differentiation, with strict watch over the particular self-interests, and last but not least with a thoroughly business-like spirit not devoid of suspicion, jealousy and mean practices.

If a concrete survey of the personal relations within the sub-clan were taken, the strained and distinctly unfriendly attitude between maternal uncle and nephew as we saw it in Omarakana, would be by no means infrequently found. Between brothers sometimes there exists real friendship, as was the case with Mitakata and his brothers, and with Namwana Guya'u and his. On the other hand, strong hatreds and acts of violence and hostility are on record both in legend and actual life. I shall give a concrete example of fatal disharmony within what should be the nucleus of a clan : a group of brothers.

In a village quite close to where I was camping at that time, there lived three brothers, the eldest of whom, the headman of the clan, was blind. The youngest brother used to take advantage of this infirmity and to gather the betel-nut from the palms even before it was properly ripe. The blind man was thus deprived of his share. One day when he discovered again that he was cheated of his due, he broke into a passion of fury, seized an axe, and entering his brother's house in the dark, he succeeded in wounding him. The wounded man escaped and took refuge in the third brother's house. This one, indignant at the outrage done to the youngest brother, took a spear and killed the blind man. The tragedy had a prosaic ending, for the murderer was put into jail for one year by the magistrate. In the olden days—on this all my informants were unanimous—he would have committed suicide.

In this case we meet the two standard criminal acts, theft and murder, combined and it will be well to make a brief digression on them. Neither delict plays any considerable part in the life of the Trobriand natives. Theft is classified under two concepts : *kwapatu* (lit. to catch hold), which word is applied to unlawful appropriation of objects of personal use, implements, and valuables ; and *vayla'u*, a special word, applied to theft of vegetable food either from gardens or yam-houses, also used when pigs or fowl are purloined. While the thieving of personal objects is felt to be a greater nuisance, stealing of food is more despicable. There is no greater disgrace to a Trobriander than to be without food, in need of it, to beg for it, and an admission by act that one has been in such straits as to steal it entails the greatest humiliation conceivable. Again, since the theft of valuables is almost out of question, because they are all earmarked,[1] thieving of personal objects cannot

[1] Cf. the writer's op. cit., *Argonauts of the Western Pacific*.

I

inflict any serious loss on the rightful owner. The
penalties in either case would consist in the shame and
ridicule which covers the culprit and, indeed, all cases
of theft brought to my notice were perpetrated by
feeble-minded people, social outcasts, or minors.
Depriving the white man of his superfluous possessions,
such as trade goods, tinned food or tobacco, which he
keeps locked in a niggardly fashion without using, is
in a class by itself, and is naturally not considered
a breach of law, morality or gentlemanly manners.

A murder is an extremely rare occurrence. In fact,
apart from the case just described, only one
occurred during my residence : the spearing of a
notorious sorcerer at night, while he was surreptitiously
approaching the village. This was done in defence of the
sick man, the victim of the sorcerer, by one of the armed
guard who keep watch during the night on such
occasions.

A few cases are told of killing as punishment for
adultery caught *in flagranti*, insults to people of high
rank, brawls and skirmishes. Also, of course, killing
during regular war. In all cases when a man is killed
by people of another sub-clan, there is the obligation
of *talion*. This, in theory, is absolute, in practice it is
regarded obligatory only in cases of a male adult of
rank or importance ; and even then it is considered
superfluous when the deceased had met his fate for a
fault clearly his own. In other cases, when vendetta

is obviously demanded by the honour of the sub-clan, it is still evaded by the substitution of blood-money (*lula*). This was a regular institution in the making of peace after war, when a compensation was given to the other side for every one killed and wounded. But also when murder or homicide were committed, a *lula* would relieve the survivors from the duty of talion (*lugwa*).

And that brings us back to the problem of clan unity. All the facts quoted above show that the unity of the clan is neither a mere fairy tale, invented by Anthropology, nor yet the one and only real principle of savage law, the key to all its riddles and difficulties. The actual state of affairs, fully seen and thoroughly understood, is very complex, full of apparent as well as of real contradictions and of conflicts due to the play of the Ideal and its actualization, to the imperfect adjustment between the spontaneous human tendencies and rigid law. The unity of the clan is a legal fiction in that it demands—in all native doctrine, that is in all their professions, and statements, sayings, overt rules and patterns of conduct—an absolute subordination of all other interests and ties to the claims of clan solidarity, while, in fact, this solidarity is almost constantly sinned against and practically non-existent in the daily run of ordinary life. On the other hand, at certain times, in the ceremonial phases of native life above all, the clan unity dominates everything and in cases of overt clash and open challenge it will overrule personal considerations and failings which under ordinary conditions would certainly determine the individual's conduct. There are, therefore, two sides to the question, and most of the important events of native life, as well as of their institutions, customs, and tendencies cannot be properly understood without the realization of both sides and of their interaction.

It is not difficult to see also, why Anthropology fixed upon one side of the question, why it presented the rigid but fictitious doctrine of native law as the whole truth. For this doctrine represents the intellectual, overt, fully conventionalized aspect of the native attitude, the one set into clear statements, into definite legal formulæ. When the native is asked what he would do in such and such a case, he answers what he *should* do ; he lays down the pattern of best possible conduct. When he acts as informant to a field-anthropologist, it costs him nothing to retail the Ideal of the law. His sentiments, his propensities, his bias, his self-indulgences as well as tolerance of others' lapses, he reserves for his behaviour in real life. And even then, though he acts thus, he would be unwilling to admit often even to himself, that he ever acts below the standard of law. The other side, the natural, impulsive code of conduct, the evasions, the compromises and non-legal usages are revealed only to the field-worker, who observes native life directly, registers facts, lives at such close quarters with his 'material' as to understand not only their language and their statements, but also the hidden motives of behaviour, and the hardly ever formulated spontaneous line of conduct. 'Hearsay Anthropology' is constantly exposed to the danger of ignoring the seamy side of savage law. This side, it can be said without exaggeration, exists and is tolerated as long as it is not squarely faced, put into words, openly stated and thus challenged. This accounts perhaps for the old theory of the 'untrammelled savage' whose customs are none and whose manners are beastly. For the authorities who gave us this version knew well the intricacies and irregularities of native behaviour which by no means conforms to strict law, while they ignored the structure of native legal doctrine. The modern field-worker constructs it without much trouble from his native informant's statements, but he remains ignorant of the blurs made by human nature on this theoretical outline. Hence he has re-shaped the savage into a model of legality. Truth is a combination of both versions and our knowledge of it reveals the old as well as the new figment as futile simplifications of a very complicated state of things.

This, like everything else in human cultural reality is not a consistent logical scheme, but rather a seething mixture of conflicting principles. Among these the clash of matriliny and paternal interest is probably the most important. The discrepancy between the totemic clan solidarity on the one hand, and the bonds of family or dictates of self-interest comes next. The struggle of the hereditary principle of rank with the personal influences of prowess, economic success and magical craft is also of importance. Sorcery as a personal instrument of power deserves special mention, for the sorcerer is often a dreaded competitor of the chief or headman. If space permitted I could give examples of other conflicts of a more concrete, accidental nature ; the historically ascertainable gradual spread of political power of the Tabalu sub-clan (of the Malasi clan), in which we can see the principle of rank override beyond its legitimate field the law of strictly local citizenship, based on mythological claims and matrilineal succession. Or else I might describe the secular contest between the same Tabalu and the Toliwaga sub-clan (of the Lukwasisiga clan), in which the former have on their side rank, prestige and established power and the latter a stronger military organization, war-like qualities and greater success in fighting.

The most important fact from our point of view in this struggle of social principles is that it forces us to re-cast completely the traditional conception of law and order in savage communities. We have to abandon now definitely the idea of an inert, solid ' crust ' or ' cake ' of custom rigidly pressing from outside upon the whole surface of tribal life. Law and order arise out of the very processes which they govern. But they are not rigid, nor due to any inertia or permanent mould. They obtain on the contrary as the result of a constant struggle not merely of human passions against the law, but of legal principles with one another. The struggle, however, is not a free fight : it is subject to definite conditions, can take place only within certain limits and only on the condition that it remains under the surface of publicity. Once an open challenge has been entered, the precedence of strict law over legalized usage or over an encroaching principle of law is established and the orthodox hierarchy of legal systems controls the issue.

For as we have seen the conflict takes place between strict law and legalized usage, and it is possible because the former has the strength of more definite tradition behind it, while the latter draws force from personal inclinations and actual power. There exist thus within the body of law not only different types such as quasi-civil and quasi-criminal, or the law of economic transactions, of political relations, etc., but there can be distinguished degrees of orthodoxy, stringency, and validity, placing the rules into a hierarchy from the main law of Mother-right, totemism, and rank down to the clandestine evasions and the traditional means of defying law and abetting crime.

Herewith our survey of law and legal institutions in the Trobriand Islands comes to an end. In its course we have reached a number of conclusions about the existence of positive and elastic and yet binding obligations, which correspond to the civil law in more developed cultures ; about the influence of reciprocity, public enactment and the systematic incidence of such obligations, which supply their main binding forces ; about the negative rulings of law, the tribal prohibitions and taboos, which we have found as elastic and adaptable as the positive rules although fulfilling a different function. We were also able to suggest a new classification of the rules of custom and tradition ; a revised definition of law as a special class of customary rules and to indicate further sub-divisions within the body of law itself. In this, besides the main division between quasi-civil and quasi-criminal we found that a distinction must be made between the various grades of law which can be arranged into a hierarchy from the statutes of main legitimate law, through legally tolerated usages down to evasions and traditional methods of flouting the law. We also had to discriminate between a number of distinct systems which together form the body of tribal law such as Mother-right and Father-love, political organization and magical influence, systems which at times enter into conflict, arrive at compromises and re-adjustments. There is no need to go further into detail about all this, for our conclusions were both substantiated with evidence and discussed theoretically at length.

But it is worth while to realize once more that throughout our discussion we found the real problem not in bald enumeration of rules, but in the ways and means by which these are carried out. Most instructive we found the study of the life situations which call for a given rule, the manner in which this is handled by the people concerned, the reaction of the community at large, the consequences of fulfilment or neglect. All this, which could be called the cultural-context of a primitive system of rules is equally important, if not more so, than the mere recital of a fictitious native *corpus juris* codified into the ethnographer's note-book as the result of question and answer, in the hearsay method of field-work.

With this we are demanding a new line of anthro-pological field-work : the study by direct observation of the rules of custom as they function in actual life. Such study reveals that the commandments of law and custom are always organically connected and not isolated ; that their very nature consists in the many tentacles which they throw out into the context of social life ; that they only exist in the chain of social trans-actions in which they are but a link. I maintain that the staccato manner in which most accounts of tribal life are given is the result of imperfect information, and that it is in fact incompatible with the general character of human life and the exigencies of social organization. A native tribe bound by a code of disconnected inorganic customs would fall to pieces under our very eyes.

We can only plead for the speedy and complete disappearance from the records of field-work of the piecemeal items of information, of customs, beliefs, and rules of conduct floating in the air, or rather leading a flat existence on paper with the third-dimension, that of life, completely lacking. With this the theoretical arguments of Anthropology will be able to drop the lengthy litanies of threaded statement, which make us anthropologists feel silly, and the savage look ridiculous. I mean by this the long enumerations of bald statement such as, for example, " Among the Brobdignacians when a man meets his mother-in-law, the two abuse each other and each retires with a black eye " ; " When a Brodiag encounters a Polar bear he runs away and sometimes the bear follows " ; " in old Caledonia when a native accidentally finds a whiskey bottle by the road-side he empties it at one gulp, after which he proceeds immediately to look for another "— and so forth. (I am quoting from memory so the statements may be only approximate, though they sound plausible.)

It is easy, however, to poke fun at the litany-method, but it is the field-worker who is really responsible. There is hardly any record in which the majority of statements are given as they occur in actuality and not as they should or are said to occur. Many of the earlier accounts were written to startle, to amuse, to be facetious at the expense of the savage, till the tables were turned and it is more easy now to be facetious at the anthropologist's expense. To the old recorders what mattered really was the queerness of the custom, not its reality. The modern anthropologist, working through an interpreter by the question and answer method can again collect only opinions, generalizations, and bald statements. He gives us no reality, for he has never seen it. The touch of ridicule which hangs about most writings of anthropology is due to the artificial flavour of a statement torn out of its life-context. The true problem is not to study how human life submits to rules—it simply does not ; the real problem is how the rules become adapted to life.

As regards our theoretical gains the analysis of Trobriand law has given us a clear view of the forces of cohesion in a primitive society, based on solidarity within the group as well as on the appreciation of personal interest. The opposition of primitive ' group-sentiment ', ' joint personality ' and ' clan absorption ' to civilized individualism and pursuit of selfish ends appear to us altogether artificial and futile. No society, however primitive or civilized, can be based on a figment or on a pathological growth on human nature.

The results of this memoir point to one more moral. Although I have confined myself principally to descriptions and statements of fact, some of these led

naturally to a more general theoretical analysis which
yielded certain explanations of the facts discussed. Yet
in all this not once was it necessary to resort to any
hypotheses, to any evolutionary or historical recon-
structions. The explanations here given consisted in
an analysis of certain facts into simpler elements and
of tracing the relations between these elements. Or
else it was possible to correlate one aspect of culture
with another and to show which is the function fulfilled
by either within the scheme of culture. The relation
between Mother-right and the paternal principle and
their partial conflict accounts, as we have seen, for a
series of compromise formations such as cross-cousin
marriage, types of inheritance and economic
transactions, the typical constellation of father, son,
and maternal uncle, and certain features of the clan
system.[1] Several characteristics of their social life, the
chains of reciprocal duties, the ceremonial enactment
of obligations, the uniting of a number of disparate
transactions into one relationship have been explained
by the function which they fulfil in supplying the
coercive forces of law. The relation between hereditary
prestige, the power of sorcery, and the influence of
personal achievement as we find them in the Trobriands
could be accounted for by the cultural parts played by
each principle respectively. While remaining on strictly

---

[1] The relation between Mother-right and Father-love is more
fully discussed in op. cit., *Sex and Repression in Savage Society.*

empirical ground we were able to account for all these facts and features, show their conditions as well as the ends which they fulfil, and thus to explain them in a scientific manner. This type of explanation by no means excludes further investigation as to the evolutionary level of such customs or as to their historical antecedents. There is room for the antiquarian interest as well as the scientific, but the former should not claim an exclusive or even predominant sway over Anthropology. It is high time that the student of Man should also be able to say *" hypotheses non fingo "*.

INDEX

Adultery, 81, 96 ; punishment, 92, 118 ; marks on corpse, 84 ; and child, 108 n.

Ambition, 29, 30, 32, 58, 67–68 ; in gardening, 36

Année Sociologique, 41 n., 57 n.

Anthropology, scientific nature, 1–2, 71–74 ; practical value, 1–2

Bachofen, 2

Baloma (v. Spirits)

Bernhöft, 2

Black Magic (v. Sorcery)

Blood money, 115, 119

Breach of law, Pt. II, Ch. I, *et passim*

Brother, and sister in Trobriand law, 35–38 ; murder of, 116–117

Canoe, ownership, 18–21 ; master and crew, 26–27

Ceremonial, display, 23, 29, 32, 36–37, 55, 67, 128 ; distribution, 34, 61, 114, 115

Chief, 46–47, 66, 76 ; power of punishment, 89–92 ; and son, 101–106, 110

Civil law among savages, 30–31, 33, 56–59, 63–68, 73–74, 123–124

Clan, 47–49, 55, 75 ; unity, 112–120, 127 ; conflict of, 122 ; (v. also Exogamy, Mother-right)

Classificatory system of relationship, 82, 113

Cohesion, forces in tribe, 112–120

Communism, primitive : concept criticized, 3, 11, 16, 18–21, 26, 48–49, 73, and Pt. I, Ch. II

Conflict of principles in law, 76, 100–111, 121–123

Conformism of savages, 52

Co-operation, 18–21, 26–27

Counter-magic, 80–81

Crime, 63, 117 ; and punishment, Pt. II ; 94, 97–99, 117–119 (v. also Criminal law)

Criminal law, 56–58, 66

Cross-cousin marriage, 110–111

Cultural context in anthropological study, 125–127

Custom, automatic submission to, Pt. I, Ch. I ; 3–4, 30, 50–52, 56, 63–68, 73, 122 ; force of, 65 ; rules of, 50–54

Dual organization, 24–25

Durkheim, 4, 55, 57 n.

Economic relations, 25–27, 35–42 ; in fishing, 17–21 ; coastal and inland, 22–23

Elasticity of law, 31, 58

European war, native view, 83 n.

Evasion, of obligations, 28, 30 ; of results of breach of law, 80–81

Exchange, 22, 23, 25–27 (v. also *Kula*)

Exhumation, 87–90

Exogamy, 77–80, 82–84

Father and son, strangers, 101, 107, 108

Fatherhood, ignorance of physiology of, 107–108 n.

Father-love, 100–111

Feasts, 114

Fieldwork methods, 120–121, 125–127

Fishing, 17–18, 20 ; motives in, 26–28